THE ANCIENT

WORD

OF

GOD

KJV ONLY OR NOT?

By Ken Johnson, Th.D.

Printed in the United States of America

ISBN 1477639896
EAN-13 978-1477639894

Contents

Master List of English Bibles

	Abbrev	Name	Date
1		Wycliffe	1382
2		Tyndale New Testament	1526
3		Coverdale	1535
4		Matthew	1537
5		Great Bible	1537
6		Taverner	1539
7		Geneva	1560
8		Bishops' Bible	1568
9	DRB	Douai-Rheims	1582
10	KJV	Authorized King James Version	1611
11	Mace	Mace New Testament	1729
12	Whiston	Whiston's Primitive New Testament	1745
13	DRC	Challoner's Revision of the R-D	1752
14		Doddridge's New Testament	1756
15	Wesley	Wesley's New Testament	1760
16	Quaker	Anthony Purver Bible	1764
17		Wakefield New Testament	1791
18		New Testament in an Improved Version	1808
19	Thm	Thomson's Translation	1808
20	JST	Joseph Smith's Translation	1830
21	Webster	Webster's Revision	1833
22	LONT	Living Oracles New Testament	1835
23	Etheridge	Etheridge's Peshitta	1849
24		Brenton's Septuagint	1851
25	Murdock	Murdock's Peshitta	1852
26	Leeser	Leeser Bible	1853
27	YLT	Young's Literal Translation	1862
28		Emphatic Diaglott	1864
29	Anderson	Anderson's 1865 New Testament	1865
30	Noyes	New Testament	1869
31	Julia	Julia E. Smith Parker Translation	1876
32	RV	Revised Version	1885
33	DBY	Darby Bible	1890
34	ASV	American Standard Version	1901
35	EBR	Rotherham's Emphasized Bible	1902
36	TCNT	The Twentieth Century New Testament	1902
37	Godbey	Godbey New Testament	1902
38	Fenton	The Holy Bible in Modern English	1903
39	WNT	Weymouth New Testament	1903
40	WAS	Worrell New Testament	1904
41	WVSS	Westminster Version of the Sacred Scriptures	1913

42	JPS	Jewish Publication Society of America Ver.	1917
43	RNT	Riverside New Testament	1923
44	MRB	Modern Reader's Bible	1923
45	CTNT	Centenary New Testament	1924
46	MNT	James Mofatt	1926
47	Lamsa	Lamsa Bible	1933
48	AAT	An American Translation	1935
49	Greber	The New Testament	1937
50	WmNT	Williams New Testament	1937
51	SPC	Spencer New Testament	1941
52	CCD	Confraternity Bible	1941
53	BBE	Bible in Basic English	1949
54	NWT	New World Translation	1950
55	RSV	Revised Standard Version	1952
56	Knox	Knox Translation of the Vulgate	1955
57	TANT	The Authentic New Testament	1955
58	HSM	Holy Scriptures of the Masoretic Text	1955
59	KLNT	Kleist-Lilly New Testament	1956
60	PME	Phillips New Testament in Modern English	1958
61	BV	The Berkeley Version	1958
62	CKJV	Children's King James Version	1960
63	WET	Wuest Expanded Translation	1961
64	NSNT	Norlie's Simplified New Testament	1961
65	TDB	The Dartmouth Bible	1961
66	NNT	Noli New Testament	1961
67	CKJV	Children's King James Bible	1962
68	HNB	Holy Name Bible	1963
69	AMP	Amplified Bible	1965
70	Knoch	Concordant Literal Version	1966
71	JB	Jerusalem Bible	1966
72	RSV-CE	Revised Standard Version Catholic Edition	1966
73		The New Testament: A New Translation	1968
74		Cotton Patch Bible	1968
75	BNT	William Barkly New Testament	1968
76	BWE	Bible in Worldwide English New Testament	1969
77	MLB	Modern Language Bible	1969
78	TBR	The Bible Reader	1969
79	NEB	New English Bible	1970
80	NAB	New American Bible	1970
81	KJII	King James II	1971
82	KJV20	KJV Twentieth Century Version	1971
83	TLB	The Living Bible	1971
84	TSB	The Story Bible	1971
85	TLB-CE	The Living Bible Catholic Edition	1971
86	NASB	New American Standard Bible	1971

87	LivEng	The Bible In Living English	1972
88	SNB	Restoration of Original Sacred Name Bible	1976
89	BECK	An American Translation	1976
90	GNB	Good News Bible	1976
91	IB	Interlinear Bible (Green)	1976
92	NIV	New International Version	1978
93	SEB	Simple English Bible	1980
94	SSBE	Sacred Scriptures Bethel Edition	1981
95	NKJV	New King James Version	1982
96		A New Accurate Translation	1984
97	NJB	New Jerusalem Bible	1985
98	NJPS	New Jewish Publication Society of America	1985
99	LITV	Green's Literal Translation	1985
100	ONT	Original New Testament	1985
101	KIT	Kingdom Interlinear Translation	1985
102	CCB	Christian Community Bible	1986
103	NLV	New Life Version	1986
104	MCT	McCord's New Testament	1988
105	NRSV	New Revised Standard Version	1989
106	NRSV-CE	New Revised Standard Version Catholic Ed.	1989
107	JNT	Jewish New Testament	1989
108	REB	Revised English Bible	1989
109	ERV	Easy-to Read Version	1989
110	GNC	God's New Covenant New Testament	1989
111	EVD	English Version for the Deaf	1989
113	KJ21	21st Century King James Version	1991
113	NCV	New Century Version	1991
114	Gaus	Unvarnished New Testament	1991
115	TEV	Today's English Bible	1992
116		Clear Word	1994
117	GW	God's Word	1995
118	CEV	Contemporary English Version	1995
119	AST	Anointed Standard Version	1995
120	AIV	An Inclusive Version	1995
121	NIrV	New International Reader's Version	1996
122	NIVI	New International Inclusive Language	1996
123		The New Testament (Lattimore)	1996
124	NLT	New Living Translation	1996
125	TMB	Third Millennium Bible	1998
126	CJB	Complete Jewish Bible	1998
127	TS98	The Scriptures '98 Version	1998
128	RcV	Recovery Version	1999
129	MKJV	Modern King James Version	1999
130	AKJV	American King James Version	1999
131	TCE	The Common Edition New Testament	1999

132	ALT	Analytical-Literal Translation	1999
133		The Last Days New Testament	1999
134	UKJV	Updated King James Version	2000
135	KJV2000	King James 2000 Version	2000
136	SSFOY	Sacred Scriptures, Family of Yah Edition	2000
137	RKJNT	Revised King James New Testament	2000
138	EEB	Easy English Bible	2001
139	KJVER	King James Version Easy Reading	2001
140	ESV	English Standard Version	2001
141	HSV	Holy Scriptures Version	2001
142		2001 Translation	2001
143	UTV	Urim Thummim Version	2001
144	WV	Wycliffe Version (Noble)	2001
145	MSG	The Message	2002
146	OJB	Orthodox Jewish Bible	2002
147		A Fresh Parenthetical Translation (NT)	2002
148	HNC	Holy New Covenant	2002
149	TWOY	The Word of Yahweh	2003
150	CKJV	Comfort-able King James Version	2003
151	EMTV	English Majority Text Version	2003
152	ABP	Apostolic Bible Polyglot	2003
153	FNT	Faithful New Testament	2003
154	VW	A Voice In The Wilderness Holy Scriptures	2003
155	CGV	Context Group Version	2003
156	HCSB	Holman Christian Standard Bible	2004
157	AB	The Apostles' Bible	2004
159	HRV	Hebraic-Roots Version	2004
160	TSNT	The Source New Testament	2004
161	Younan	Younan's Peshitta Interlinear	2004
162	NSB	New Simplified Bible	2004
163	TNIV	Today's New International Version	2005
164	NET	New English Translation	2005
165	NCPB	New Cambridge Paragraph Bible	2005
166	SN-KJ	Sacred Name King James Bible	2005
167	KJ3	KJ3—Literal Translation Bible	2005
168	CAB	Complete Apostles' Bible	2005
169	ACV	A Conservative Version	2005
170		Renovaré Spiritual Formation Bible	2005
171		Life With God Study Bible	2005
172	WNT	William's New Testament	2005
173	UVNT	Understandable Version NT	2005
174	ChB	Christolog Bible	2005
175	ARTB	Ancient Roots Translinear Bible	2006
176	AV7	AV7 (New Authorized Version)	2006
177	AVU	Authorized Version Update	2006

178		Spirit of Prophecy Study Bible	2006
179	NETS	New English Translation of the Septuagint	2007
180	OSB	Orthodox Study Bible	2007
181	ICB	International Children's Bible	2007
182	NIBEV	Natural Israelite Bible, English Version	2007
183	TB	The Besorah (plagiarized '98 version)	2008
184	COM	The Comprehensive New Testament	2008
185		The Voice	2008
186	NHEB	New Heart English Bible	2008
187	HOB	Holy Orthodox Bible	2008
188	TNB	Tarish Nephite Bible	2008
189	ANT	Accurate New Testament	2008
190	CPDV	Catholic Public Domain Version	2009
191	UPDV	Updated Version	2009
192	WGCIB	Work of God's Children Illustrated Bible	2010
193	OEB	Open English Bible	2010
194	NIV10	NIV 2010	2010
195	LEB	Lexham English Bible	2010
196	EOB	Eastern / Greek Orthodox Bible	2010
197	TFB	The Free Bible	2010
198	NABRE	New American Bible Revised Edition	2011
199	MLV	Modern Literal Version	2011
200	DB	Disciple's Bible	2011
201	EB	Expanded Bible	2011
202	TrLB	Tree of Life Bible	2011
203	WEB	World English Bible	-
204	WEB-ME	World English Bible Messianic Edition	-
205	HNV	Hebrew Names Version	-
206	CBP	Conservative Bible Project	-
207	DRP	David Robert Palmer Translation	-
208	RNKJV	Restored Name King James Version	-
209	MGB	The Manga Bible	-
210	ISV	International Standard Version	-
211	Jubilee	English Jubilee 2000 Bible	-
212	YRT	Young's Revised Translation	-
213	FAA	Far Above All Version	-
214	Szasz	Awful New Testament (Emery Szasz)	-
215	MASV	Modern American Standard Version	-
216	TEB	Transparent English Bible	-
217		The Victorious Gospel of Jesus Christ New Covenant Translation	-

- Internet based or not yet published

Inspiration of Scripture

In an effort to get a clear picture of why we have so many Bibles, we first created a master list showing 217 English Bibles. We will first look briefly at their history. Next we will look at what languages they were translated from, which manuscripts were reliable and which had numerous errors. Finally, we will look at which people, societies, denominations, or cults created these Bibles and what they may have been trying to do with the text.

Hopefully, when we end this study, you will understand why an accurate Bible is so important and be able to continue to see, as new Bibles come out, which are good Bibles to use and which ones are not.

Inspiration and Inerrancy
The apostle Paul states that *all* Scripture is inspired, which means God wrote exactly what He wanted though the hand of the prophet or apostle. Therefore God gave each verse in the Scripture for us to know what we are supposed to do or not do and to tell us what God is doing now and what will happen in the future.

All Scripture *is* given by inspiration of God, and *is* profitable for doctrine, for reproof, for correction, for instruction in righteousness: that the man of God may be perfect, thoroughly furnished unto all good works. *2 Timothy 3:16-17*

The apostle Peter explained that prophecy proves Scripture is inspired. No mere human being can predict what will happen in the future with one hundred percent accuracy.

> Knowing this first, that no prophecy of the Scripture is of any private interpretation. For the prophecy came not in old time by the will of man: but holy men of God spake *as they were* moved by the Holy Ghost. *2 Peter 1:20-21*

This also means that the prophet or apostle knew when he was writing something inspired by God and when he was not. Only the inspired writings were placed in the canon of Scripture. The sixty-six books of the Old and New Testaments comprise the inspired Word of God. The apostle Paul warned us that it was not the *apostles* that were inspired, but their *writings*.

> And these things, brethren, I have in a figure transferred to myself and *to* Apollos for your sakes; that ye might learn in us not to think *of men* above that which is written, that no one of you be puffed up for one against another.
> *1 Corinthians 4:6*

Prophecy

Since Peter wrote that prophecy proves the whole Bible is inspired, we should look at a few prophecies to see exactly what he meant. Isaiah 12:2-3 states the name of the Messiah will be "Salvation."

Behold, God *is* my salvation; I will trust, and not be afraid: for the LORD JEHOVAH *is* my strength and *my* song; he also is become my salvation. Therefore with joy shall ye draw water out of the wells of salvation. *Isaiah 12:2-3*

The Hebrew word used in this passage for salvation is *Yeshua*. Yeshua is translated into English as "Joshua;" and when translated into Greek, then into English, as "Jesus."

And there shall come forth a rod out of the stem of Jesse, and a Branch shall grow out of his roots: *Isaiah 11:1*

Isaiah 11:1 records that the title of the Messiah will be "The Branch." The Hebrew word for branch in this passage is *Natzer*. Matthew 2:23 reveals that this was a prophecy that Jesus would be called a Nazarene.

And he came and dwelt in a city called Nazareth: that it might be fulfilled which was spoken by the prophets, He shall be called a Nazarene. *Matthew 2:23*

These same terms come up again in Zechariah 3:8-10.

Hear now, O Joshua the high priest, thou, and thy fellows that sit before thee: for they are men wondered at: for, behold, I will bring forth my servant the BRANCH. For behold the stone that I have laid before Joshua; upon one stone shall be seven eyes: behold, I will engrave the graving thereof, saith the LORD of hosts, and I will remove the iniquity of that land in one day. In that day, saith the LORD of hosts, shall ye call every man his neighbour under the vine and under the fig tree. *Zechariah 3:8-10*

Joshua the high priest represents the Messiah when God calls him "My Branch." So we see *Yeshua HaNazari*, or Jesus of Nazareth, being predicted. He is sitting on a throne between his two appearances. This corresponds to Jesus sitting at the right hand of the Father during the church age. There is a seven-sided stone at his feet with an inscription on it. The inscription is a very important prophecy but we are not given the inscription. Or are we? Verse 8 says Joshua and his friends are the sign (thing wondered at). In other words, their names are the inscription. This is the same kind of riddle that Daniel interpreted by reading the handwriting on the wall. When we gather the names of the individuals and string them together their names actually form a sentence. Their names and meanings are: Heldi (age), Tobijah (Yahweh is good), Jedaiah (Yahweh's news), Hen (grace), Zephaniah (Yahweh prepared), Josiah (foundation), Zephaniah[a] (Yahweh has hidden), Helem (pierced one), Joshua (Salvation), Jehozedek (cleanses), Zerubabbal (the Lord infills), Shialtiel (God's charge laid up). The inscription is:

---

[a] Zephaniah cane be translated either "Yahweh has hidden" or "Yahweh has prepared."

Yahweh has prepared the age of the Gospel (good news) of grace, hidden from the foundation of the world, that by the pierced one's salvation, we should be cleansed from the charge God laid up against us and infilled with the Lord's (Spirit).

I believe Jesus was referring to this inscription prophecy in Matthew 13:35 when he mentioned things "kept secret from the foundation of the world." My book *Ancient Prophecies Revealed* describes numerous prophecies like these.

Plenary Verbal Inspiration
What can we learn about inspiration from these prophecies?

1. Would it matter that a word was misspelled or had an alternate spelling, as long as we could tell what the word was? No.

   Some people love to search the letters of Scripture and look for what is commonly called Bible codes. The ancient church fathers stated that they were taught by the apostles that if Scripture suggested you look at a letter code (like 666 in Revelation), then look at it; but to randomly look for possible hidden codes is, at best, a waste of time.

   Would you rather spend hours looking for things that are not there or find more inscription prophesies like the one above?

2. Would it matter if the words or phrases were flipped around like we see in the New Testament (eg. Christ Jesus or Jesus Christ)? No, in the prophetic riddle given above the words were flipped around. That was part of the riddle.

3. Would it matter if a different word replaced one of the words in the sentence (like "went away" to "walked away" or "left")? No, as long as the different word gave the same meaning.

4. Would it matter if we left out extra words in a sentence like "the" or "who?" Possibly. Some Greek words are not translated into English; but we need to be able to refer back to them.

5. Would it matter if a verse was missing a clause or a whole sentence? Yes!!!!

So the first thing we should do is to see if there are any Bibles that have missing verses, clauses, or words. Then we decide if their exclusion changes any Bible prophecy. We will do this in the following chapters, starting with the history of the Greek and Hebrew texts of the Bible.

Preservation

We know God literally wrote the Scripture through the apostles and prophets. This is obvious when we consider the fifty-four prophecies that have been fulfilled since Israel was re-established as a state in AD 1948. Even the date of Israel's return was predicted and fulfilled with one hundred percent accuracy!

With this in mind, what would happen if God allowed His inspired word to be corrupted? The purpose for it would be nullified and God's time wasted. Jesus said this would never happen. Obviously God has supernaturally protected the very words of Scripture!

> For verily I say unto you, Till heaven and earth pass, one jot or one tittle shall in no wise pass from the law, till all [prophecies] be fulfilled. *Matthew 5:18*

The phrase "jot and tittle" is an idiom meaning "not one word." Jesus defined this in Luke.

> And He said unto them, These *are* the **words** which I spake unto you, while I was yet with you, that all things must be fulfilled, which were written in the law of Moses, and *in* the prophets, and *in* the psalms, concerning Me. *Luke 24:44*

John 10:35 says "the Scripture cannot be broken," which means there are no contradictions in Scripture. Psalm 105:8 promises that God will preserve His Word "to a thousand generations." Psalm 12:6-7 and other Scriptures declare that God will preserve His Word unto all generations. Jesus said:

> Heaven and earth shall pass away, but My words shall not pass away. *Matthew 24:35*

When Jesus said "My words," He was not referring to differences in spelling or transposed words, but the meaning of *each individual word*. So we need a word-for-word Bible translation. Isaiah 40:8 says "the word of our God shall stand forever." Peter quotes this entire verse, then applies it to the gospel.

> For all flesh *is* as grass, and all the glory of man as the flower of grass. The grass withereth, and the flower thereof falleth away: but the word of the Lord endureth for ever. And this is the word which by the gospel is preached unto you.
> *1 Peter 1:24-25*

Peter is saying that the "word" Isaiah was referring to was the prophecies that were written in the Old Testament. He and the other apostles were teaching that these prophecies prove Jesus is the prophesied Messiah. Therefore, the Word of God that will be preserved forever is the written Bible.

> For whatsoever things were written aforetime were written for our learning, that we through patience and comfort of the Scriptures might have hope. *Romans 15:4*

If the "word" that will endure forever was "written for our learning," it follows then that it must be preserved here on earth. Otherwise, it will not accomplish its task!

> For I testify unto every man that heareth the words of the prophecy of this book, If any man shall add unto these things, God shall add unto him the plagues that are written in this book: and if any man shall take away from the words of the book of this prophecy, God shall take away his part out of the book of life, and out of the holy city, and *from* the things which are written in this book. *Revelation 22:18-19*

Notice Revelation declares that anyone who obscures the written prophecies by either adding to, or taking away, words, phrases, clauses, or whole sentences, will be punished severely. This refers to the "prophecies" not just contained in the book of Revelation, but throughout the whole Bible.

The ancient rabbis taught the inspiration of Scripture. Their history book, the Seder Olam, states:

> The old sages taught everyone who abandons the teaching of the Scriptures, those who deny the resurrection of the physical body, those who say that the Bible is not the inspired word of God, and those who scoff at the words of the prophets, will suffer in hell forever. *Seder Olam 3*

Ancient Word of God

The ancient church fathers who wrote before AD 325 warned us that in the end times people inside the church would rise up and reject the prophecies, despise Scripture, and deny its impartation.

[In the end times] the temples of God will be like houses, and there will be overturnings of the churches everywhere. The Scriptures will be despised, and everywhere they will sing the songs of the adversary... from among those who profess to be Christians will rise up then false prophets, false apostles, deceivers who do not recognize the inspiration of Scripture... *Hippolytus*

When the Messiah's coming is at hand, his disciples will forsake the teaching of the twelve apostles and their faith, their love and their purity... And in those days there will be many who... are devoid of wisdom, and the Holy Spirit will depart from many... And they will set aside the prophecies of the prophets...
Church father Isaiah, *AOI Fragment*

The Armenian Church preserved what they believe is *Third Corinthians*, written by Paul. It states that before the Second Coming people will deliberately falsify the words of Jesus. In this last century this has been done through the vast number of corrupt Bibles that have been printed.

My Lord Jesus Christ will come quickly when He
is rejected by those who falsify His words.
3 Corinthians 2:3

Conclusion

God supernaturally inspired the Bible and will continue to
supernaturally preserve its words because it contains
prophecy which proves He is in control and we can obtain
the free gift of salvation. He will also allow cults to
tamper with His words and create their own corrupt
Bibles; but they will be damned for doing this. In the next
chapter we will look at the history of the Bible and see
how the cults and their corruption began.

Ancient Word of God

Bible History

The doctrine of the Apostles has been guarded as a very complete system of doctrine and has been preserved without any forging of Scriptures. Neither receive addition to, nor suffer curtailment from, its truths. Read the Word of God without falsification, lawfully and diligently explaining the Old Testament in harmony with the rest of the Scriptures.
Irenaeus *Against Heresies 4.33*, AD 178

The ancient church believed the Bible was inspired and perfect. They were to carefully guard it from those who would tamper with the text. Let's see how all this began.

AD 32-132
Acts 11:26-27 teaches that believers in Messiah were first called Christians in Antioch and that the prophets frequented Antioch in the early days.

The last book of the Bible, Revelation, was written about AD 95 by the apostle John when he had been banished to the Island of Patmos for being a Christian. In AD 96, John was released from his prison and returned to the city of Ephesus, using it as a headquarters for missionary work. John and Polycarp continued to plant churches for the next twenty years. Meanwhile, the scribes at Antioch continued to produce copies of the inspired writings of the apostles. They were eventually grouped together to form the New Treatment.

Mark took his gospel and set up the Christian church in Alexandria, Egypt. He was martyred there. While the Essenes of Qumran were producing the Dead Sea Scrolls, another Essene community developed in Egypt. The Egyptian Essenes combined Judaism and paganism. From them arose the cult of Theripute. These Theripute mixed the pagan practices of the Egyptian Essenes with Christianity. Many other Gnostic cults arose after them. Cults like the Encritites, Ebionites, and Marcionites all created their own Scriptures by *cutting out parts of the true New Testament they did not like.* They primarily cut out references to the deity of Christ, His pre-existence, and His connection to the Old Testament of the Jews. They usually worshiped many gods, or "creator angels," as they called them. The Carpocratian Gnostics were the first to introduce idolatry into their corrupt Christianity.

AD 132-200

In the second century, missionaries from Antioch took the Greek New Testament to various countries and helped those people translate Bibles into their own languages. Speaking of the gift of languages which started on the day of Pentecost, ancient church records state:

> ...according to the tongue every one of them had received, so did he prepare himself to go to that

country in which that tongue was spoken.
Ancient Church Fathers p. 173

When Irenaeus became the bishop of Lyons, France, in AD 177, the previous bishop Pothinus (87-177) had already given the local people the New Testament in their local language; the Gallic Bible[b]. Several other ethnic groups have similar legends. The missionaries taught the local people and helped them translate the pure Greek New Testament into Syriac, old Latin, Sahidic and Bohairic Coptic[c], Italic, Gallic, Goth, Armenian, Palestinian Syriac, and others.

By the mid third century, the Gnostics were stamped out everywhere but Egypt, which was the last Gnostic stronghold. A Christian named Pantinus started a school / seminary in Alexandria, Egypt. After a time Pantinus decided to resign as head of the Alexandrian school and move to the mountains. Clement of Alexandria was elected the new head of the school; but he felt uneasy about certain things he saw in the school (we are not told what they were). He decided to find Pantinus and ask him some questions. Clement finally found Pantinus living in a cave up in the mountains. Pantinus reassured Clement that nothing was wrong, so Clement took control of the school. During his time at the school in Alexandria, he wrote much commentary. His quotes of Scripture often resemble the Alexandrian text (abbreviated CT) instead of

---

[b] Legend says the Gallic Bible was translated in AD 157.
[c] All these exhibit the Received Text except the Coptic. See appendix on *Other Language Bibles*.

the Received Text (abbreviated TR or RT). For example in quoting John 1:18, he called Jesus the "only begotten God," rather than the "only begotten Son." Clement also seems to teach a kind of preterism[d] by linking some of the Revelation prophesies with the destruction of the temple in Jerusalem. This would be a common Gnostic idea, since Gnostics hated anything Jewish and thought the God of the Old Testament was a corrupt tyrant.

AD 200-325

Origen replaced Clement as head of the School of Alexandria. Origen seemed to be a great scholar, but in time was charged with teaching the heresy today known as Origenism[e]. He left the school and came to reside in Caesarea. Under his direction, copies of the Alexandrian Scripture, which he had brought with him from Egypt, were mingled with the standard Byzantine New Testament. This is where the Caesarian Text family gets its name.

By AD 325 Constantine was on the throne and Christianity was the official religion. These proceedings were recorded by Eusebius Pamphilius, known as the father of church history. Constantine ordered fifty Bibles to be created for the providences[f]. It is thought that the

---

[d] Preterism is the belief that the prophecies about the millennium are symbolic of the destruction of Jerusalem back in AD 70.

[e] Orgenism comprises the false doctrines of reincarnation, that there is no eternal hell, and there will be a universal salvation of all humans and Satan and his fallen angels.

[f] Eusebius' *Life of Constantine*

Codex Sinaiticus was one of those Bibles. If this is true, that would explain how the Latin Bibles became corrupt.

AD 325-400

Jerome was asked to create a modern version of the Bible in the common language of the people. He agreed and produced the Latin Vulgate. Jerome strongly recommended the Apocrypha be left out because it was not in the Hebrew version, and the Greek version that had it seemed corrupted. He also stated the Greek version had removed 1 John 5:7-8. He strongly opposed removing these verses from the Vulgate[g].

400-1384

During this period, the common people were discouraged from, and finally forbidden, to read the Word of God for themselves. The Latin Vulgate became more and more corrupt, as did the Roman Catholic Church. People began to rise up to reform the Catholic Church and most were martyred for their stand.

1384-1611

In 1384 Wycliffe published his Wycliffe Bible based on the Latin Vulgate. It was a good start towards getting the Bible into the hands of the people in their own native language. He died for his service. As more freedom was gained, others researched more of the old reliable Greek Scriptures and the ancient Bibles translated from the original Greek into various languages. These men labored

---

[g] Jerome's commentary on the General Epistles.

hard to translate the pure Word of God as received from the apostles and prophets into the language of the common people.

Renowned Greek scholar Erasmus took the best Greek manuscripts of his day, about twelve in all, and traveled all over Europe examining other ancient Greek manuscripts and fragments. He had other scholars check other Greek, Old Latin, Vulgate, and manuscripts written in other languages.

In 1521 Erasmus contacted a man named Bombasius in the Vatican who supplied him with readings from the Vaticanus showing that it did not contain John 4:1-3 or 1John 5:7-8. The Codex Vaticanus was discovered in the Vatican library in 1481. In 1533 Erasmus contacted another acquaintance in the Vatican, Sepúlveda, who cross-checked Erasmus' New Testament with the Vulgate and the Codex Vaticanus. Sepúlveda supplied him with a list of 365 points of difference. Erasmus decided that since the Vaticanus agreed so much with the Vulgate, it was hopelessly corrupt and rejected it entirely.

In 1522 the third edition of Erasmus' Greek text was published. It included 1 John 5:7-8.

Stefanus, a printer from Paris, took Erasmus' text and made some changes (in punctuation, typeset, etc.) and published his official Received Text in 1550 in Geneva.

In 1560 the Geneva Bible was published based on Stefanus' Received Text. The King James Bible, based on the Received Text, was published in 1611.

1611-2011

Cyril Lucar, patriarch of Alexandria, presented the Codex Alexandrinus to King James I in 1624.

In 1657 Brian Walton published a polyglot (a Bible text in more than one language side by side) based on Stephanus' Received Text, but added Codex Alexandrinus. This was the first time *ever* that there was a mixture of Greek manuscript families.

John Mill edited the Received Text and added patristic (ancient church fathers) quotes in 1707. There are over 86,000 Scripture quotes from the Ante-Nicene church fathers (AD 32-325). These quotes show the verses normally not found in modern Bibles, like 1 John 5:7-8, were included in Bibles in the second century.

Tischendorf discovered the Codex Sinaiticus at St. Catherine's Monastery in 1844. In 1881 a team led by Westcott and Hort started their revision based on the Sinaiticus and Vaticanus. Through this last century as more Alexandrian-type fragments were found, the Critical Text was developed. It is eclectic, or constantly changing. It has gone through twenty-seven revisions in the last century. The current edition is called the NA27. See the chapter on *The Critical Text (CT)* for a comparison of the missing verses.

Conclusion

We have learned what the Bible itself says about its own inspiration and preservation. We have learned the history of the Bible and its manuscripts and translations over the past two thousand years. At this point we need to look briefly at the major English Bibles and use three Old Testament verses and four New Testament verses to see how they hold up in light of Bible Prophecy. This is what the apostle Peter meant when he said that prophecy proves inspiration.

LXX and Vulgate Old Testament

Legend has it that about 250 BC seventy scholars translated the Hebrew Old Testament into Greek. This translation was called the Septuagint, abbreviated LXX, which are the Roman numerals for seventy. Ancient church father Origen tells the story of how Gnostic cults tampered with the LXX to create an Old Testament that eliminated the prophecies about Jesus the Messiah. Three people succeeded in creating and propagating their own corrupt LXX. In AD 126, Aquila, who said Jesus was not the Messiah, made changes to some of the major messianic prophecies such as Daniel 9. Later, a man named Symmachus, who denied Jesus' divinity, created his own LXX. Finally, a man named Theodotion polished Symmachus' version to make it more presentable. Theodotion was an Ebonite Gnostic.

Origen said it was easy to tell a corrupt version from the original. In about AD 240 he created what is called the Hexapla. It was a parallel Old Testament in six columns: the first column is the Hebrew Old Testament written in Hebrew characters. The second column is the Hebrew Old Testament written in Greek characters. The third column is Aquila's LXX; the forth is Symmachus' LXX; the fifth is supposed to be the original; the sixth is Theodotion's LXX. Unfortunately, the Hexapla no longer exists.

Ancient Word of God

Origen's Hexapla

Heb/Heb	Heb/Grk	Aquila	Symmachus	Original	Theodotion
בראשית	ιουδας δε	εως ιησου	εως ιησου	εως ιησου	εως ιησου
ברא אלהים	εγεννησεν	χριστου	χριστου	χριστου	χριστου
את השמים	τον φαρες	υιου δαβιδ	υιου δαβιδ	υιου δαβιδ	υιου δαβιδ
ואת הארץ:	και τον	υιου	υιου	υιου	υιου
והארץ	ζαρα εκ	αβρααμ	αβρααμ	αβρααμ	αβρααμ
היתה תהו	της θαμαρ	αβρααμ	αβρααμ	αβρααμ	αβρααμ
ובהו וחשך	φαρες δε	εγεννησεν	εγεννησεν	εγεννησεν	εγεννησεν
על-פני	εγεννησεν	τον ισαακ	τον ισαακ	τον ισαακ	τον ισαακ
תהום ורוח	τον εσρωμ	ισαακ δε	ισαακ δε	ισαακ δε	ισαακ δε
אלהים	εσρωμ δε	εγεννησεν	εγεννησεν	εγεννησεν	εγεννησεν
מרחפת	εγεννησεν	τον ιακωβ	τον ιακωβ	τον ιακωβ	τον ιακωβ
על-פני	τον αραμ	ιακωβ δε	ιακωβ δε	ιακωβ δε	ιακωβ δε
המים:	αραμ δε	εγεννησεν	εγεννησεν	εγεννησεν	εγεννησεν
ויאמר	εγεννησεν	τον ιουδαν	τον ιουδαν	τον ιουδαν	τον ιουδαν
אלהים יהי	τον	και τους	και τους	και τους	και τους
אור	αμιναδαβ	αδελφους	αδελφους	αδελφους	αδελφους
		αυτου	αυτου	αυτου	αυτου

The easiest way to check an LXX to see if it is correct is to compare the ages of the patriarchs from Adam to Noah from Genesis 5. When added up, these numbers give us the total number of years from Creation to the Flood. The numbers differ significantly.

The question is often asked: how do we know the Hebrew Old Testament is correct and not the LXX? The answer is simple. The Hebrew Old Testament refers to the ancient history *Book of Jasher* (translated the *Book of the Upright*) in Joshua 10:13, but this reference has been removed from the Septuagint. However, in 2 Samuel 1:18 (called 2 Kings in the Septuagint) both the Septuagint and the Hebrew Old Treatment record the *Book of Jasher* as being an accurate history book.

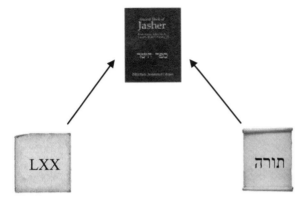

Since we have both the Greek and Hebrew Old Testaments referring to this ancient history book, we compare its dates and see which Bible it agrees with.

	Fathers Age When 1st Son Born			
	Hebrew	Jasher	LXX	Vulgate
Adam				
Seth	130	130	230	130
Enos	105	105	205	105
Kenan	90	90	190	90
Mahalalel	70	70	170	70
Jered	65	65	165	65
Enoch	162	162	162	162
Methuselah	65	65	165	65
Lamech	187	187	167	187
Noah	182	182	188	182
The Flood	600	600	600	600
Total	1656	1656	2242	1658

As we can see, ancient history agrees with the Hebrew version of the Old Treatment. Jasher disagrees with the LXX and the Latin Vulgate.

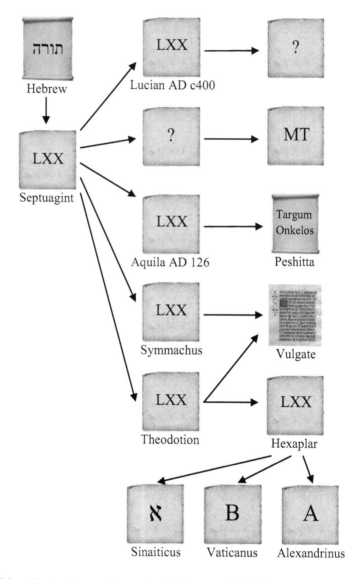

This chart shows how the Hebrew Old Testament was translated into Greek (LXX) and how the cultic versions became the basis for the Sinaiticus, Vaticanus, Alexandrinus, The Peshitta, and the Vulgate. The debased

Sinaiticus and Vaticanus are the basis for the Wescott-Hort Text, which in turn is the basis for the Critical Text, *from which most modern English Bibles are based.*

There is a paragraph in the Sinaiticus, immediately following Ezra, which notes that this text was given to Pamphilius (Eusebius) from Origen.

Prophecy

Since 2 Peter 1:20-21 states prophecy proves inspiration, let's look at how the LXX has confused just eight prophecies. See *Ancient Prophecies Revealed* for full details.

1. Isa. 11:11 (Heb) second time (CT) *omitted*
2. Obed. 20 - (Heb) Sepharad - Spain (LXX) Ephratah
3. Mic. 5:1 - (Heb) judge of Israel (LXX) tribes of Israel
4. Mic. 5:5 - (Heb) principle men (LXX) strikes
5. Dan. 5:25 - (Heb) Mene Mene (LXX) Mene
6. Dan. 9:26 - (Heb) Messiah cut off (LXX) charisma
7. Dan. 11:45 - (Heb) no one will rescue (LXX) one will rescue
8. Isa. 11:1 - (Heb) Branch - Nazari (LXX) flower

Isaiah 11:11 starts a series of prophecies that begins when Israel returns from the Roman exile (AD 1948). The LXX leaves out the most important "second time," which would make us think is it referring to the return from Babylon (536 BC).

And it shall come to pass in that day, *that* the Lord shall set his hand again <u>the second time</u> to

> recover the remnant of his people, which shall be left, from Assyria, and from Egypt, and from Pathros, and from Cush, and from Elam, and from Shinar, and from Hamath, and from the islands of the sea. *Isaiah 11:11*

Obadiah describes when, after a future war, descendants of the Jews who fled to Spain when Jerusalem was destroyed will return and settle in the Negev. The LXX replaces Sepharad (Spain) with Ephratah where Bethlehem is located. Would Jews facing impending death in Jerusalem flee to Bethlehem (six miles southwest of Jerusalem), or Spain?

> And the captivity of this host of the children of Israel *shall possess* that of the Canaanites, *even* unto Zarephath; and the captivity of Jerusalem, which *is* in Sepharad, shall possess the cities of the south. *Obadiah 1:20*

Micah predicted the Romans would smite the judge of Israel (Jesus) on the face (fulfilled in Matthew 27:26, 30). The LXX changes this to the Romans would smite the *tribes* of Israel.

> Now gather thyself in troops, O daughter of troops: he hath laid siege against us: they shall smite the judge of Israel with a rod upon the cheek. *Micah 5:1*

Micah 5:5 predicts the wars between Israel and Syria which occur after the second return of Isaiah 11. Half of these have already been fulfilled (AD 1948-1981). The LXX changes the eight principle men to "strikes."

> And this *man* shall be the peace, when the Assyrian shall come into our land: and when he shall tread in our palaces, then shall we raise against him seven shepherds, and eight principal men. *Micah 5:5*

Daniel 5 uses the handwriting on the wall to predict the judgment of Belshazzar and Babylon; but it is also a double-fulfillment prophecy that predicts the exact date of the second return to be May 14, AD 1948! The LXX removes the first "Mene," losing the time-line part of the inscription prophecy forever.

> And this *is* the writing that was written, MENE, MENE, TEKEL, UPHARSIN. *Daniel 5:25*

Daniel 9:6 predicts the death of the Messiah. While the LXX correctly has "the Messiah" in the previous verse, it changes the word "messiah" here into "charisma."

> And after threescore and two weeks shall Messiah be cut off, but not for himself: and the people of the prince that shall come shall destroy the city and the sanctuary; and the end thereof *shall be* with a flood, and unto the end of the war desolations are determined. *Daniel 9:26*

The LXX has Daniel 11:45 predicting the Antichrist will not be destroyed, but will be delivered by a mysterious person.

> And he shall plant the tabernacles of his palace between the seas in the glorious holy mountain; yet he shall come to his end, and <u>none</u> shall help him. *Daniel 11:45*

Isaiah 11:1 prophesied that the Messiah would be called a Nazarene. The word for Nazarene is *Natzer* in Hebrew. It is translated "branch" in the KJV. The LXX changes this word to "flower," completely missing the point, veiling the prophecy forever.

> And there shall come forth a rod out of the stem of Jesse, and a <u>Branch</u> shall grow out of his roots: *Isaiah 11:1*

These are just a few examples of the corruption found in all current copies of the LXX.

Fragments of what is believed to be the Lucian[h] Greek Old Testament show that they were much closer to the Hebrew Old Testament than the LXX found in the Codex Sinaiticus.

Vulgate Old Testament
In AD 382 Pope Damasus I commissioned Jerome to make a revision of the old Latin Scriptures (written in the

[h] manuscript boc2e2

high Latin of the Courts) into the common Latin (vulgar or vulgate) of the people. To be thorough, Jerome used the LXX from Origen's Hexapla (the fifth column) and Theodotion's LXX. He also used the Hebrew and Aramaic of some of the Old Testament books.

This is how the old Latin Scriptures were replaced by the common Latin Scriptures based on inferior corrupted Greek manuscripts from Alexandria. This can be easily shown by comparing the prophecies and genealogies mentioned on pages 30 and 32. We can see most are corrected to agree with the Hebrew; but, there are still major errors in the text, such as prophecies 5 and 8.

It is interesting to note that Jerome highly recommended that the Old Testament *not* include the Apocrypha because of the errors contained in it and the fact that it was not included in the Hebrew Old Testament.

These are just a few reasons why an accurate Bible should be translated from the Hebrew for the Old Testament and from the Greek for the New Testament. We should avoid texts from other languages, like the Latin vulgate, Greek Septuagint, and the Syriac, Aramaic, or other languages.

Hebrew

It may surprise some believers; but there are *two* Hebrew Old Testaments. The one the Reformers used, and is the basis for the KJV, is called the Ben Chayyim text. It is also called the "Bomberg Text" and the Second Great Rabbinic Bible (AD 1524-25). The Ben Asher text, found in the Leningrad Codex (AD 1008) is an older version and used partly in the NKJV. These two texts differ in only the nine places listed below. These make no doctrinal difference.

1. 1 Kings 20:38 - (BC) ashes on his face (BA) a bandage over his eyes.
2. Prov. 8:16 - (BC) of the earth (BA) of righteousness
3. Isa. 10:16 - (BC) Lord of hosts (BA) the LORD
4. Isa. 27:2 - (BC) red wine (BA) choice vineyard
5. Isa. 38:14 - (BC) LORD (BA) Lord
6. Jer. 34:1 - (BC) against 2x (BA) against 1x
7. Eze. 30:18 - (BC) refrained (BA) darkened
8. Zeph. 3:15 - (BC) see (BA) fear
9. Mal. 1:12 - (BC) LORD (BA) Lord

Joshua 21:36-37 is missing in the Leningrad Codex, which is a Ben Asher text, but it appears in earlier editions of all known Ben Asher and Ben Chayyim texts.

Conclusion

We have seen that ancient history agrees only with the Hebrew Old Testament; and we need a Bible that has the Old Testament translated from the Hebrew for our main study Bible.

The Majority Text (MT)

The Received Text, or Textus Receptus, abbreviated TR, is the official Greek New Testament used by the Protestant Reformers and the King James Version Bible.

The official Greek New Testament used by the Greek-speaking orthodox churches is the *Authorized Greek New Testament of the Ecumenical Patriarchate of Constantinople*, published in AD 1904. Both the TR and the official Greek text include 1 John 5:7-8.

The official Constantinople Greek New Testament used to be called the Majority Text, but in AD 1910 Hermann von Soden produced a new New Testament based on the majority of manuscripts that he could collect. This work called the *Die Schriften des neuen Testaments, in ihrer ältesten erreichbaren Textgestalt* was based on approximately eight percent of the Byzantine texts extant.

In 1985 Zane Hodges and Arthur Farstad published *The Greek New Testament According to the Majority Text* which was based on Von Soden's work.

In 1991 Maurice Robinson and William Pierpont published the *The New Testament in the Original Greek According to the Byzantine/Majority Textform.* It is similar to Hodges and Farstad's work but with more manuscripts added to the references.

In Hodges and Farstad's 2005 re-release, they state that the majority of Byzantine manuscripts are of the twelfth century or later, and therefore are ignored when considering what the original meaning was meant to be. Here is a part of that paragraph from page xiv.

> Although the far greater numerical quantity of Byzantine manuscripts (approaching 80%) exists among the documents of the twelfth and later centuries, the readings of the Byzantine Textform almost always are fully established from the earlier Byzantine lines of transmission that extend though the eleventh century. The documents of the twelfth century and later centuries generally are irrelevant to the establishment of primary Byzantine readings, and at best serve only a confirmatory purpose.

Hodges and Farstad are doing the same thing that the Critical Text people are doing. The modern "official" Majority Text is based only upon a *minority* of the available Byzantine manuscripts.

These two Majority Texts are nearly identical; but their few differences are very important. For example, the MT has "fire" omitted from Matthew 3:11, while the TR and the Constantinople Greek Text both contain "fire." Let us examine just a few of the altered passages and determine how they change doctrine.

Gambling For Jesus' Garment

John 19:24 records this event occurring and that it was a fulfillment of Old Testament prophecy (Ps. 22:18). It is also recorded in Matthew 27:35. The MT has removed the entire verse from its book of Matthew.

Jesus is the Only Son of God

Acts 8:37 records Philip saying you can become a Christian only if you believe Jesus is the Son of God. This passage is removed from the MT, probably under the influence of Gnostics who taught everyone is a child of God and Jesus was not special in this way.

The Blood of Jesus

The MT cuts out the phrase "though His Blood" from Colossians 1:14. This implies the blood Jesus shed on the cross had nothing to do with our salvation. One of the Gnostic teachings is that Jesus Christ never died on the cross. This is the same teaching held by Muslims today.

Salvation

In Revelation 21:24 we are told only "them which are saved" make it through to the millennium and into God's Kingdom. The MT removes "of them which are saved," implying that unsaved people make it into the millennium and continue to practice their sin.

See Appendix A for a list of similar problems with the Majority Text.

Ancient Word of God

The Critical Text (CT)

With the discovery of the Codex Sinaiticus and Codex Vaticanus, modern scholarship forgot about the church's historical record that taught the ancient cults *cut out* portions of Scripture, creating corrupt New Testaments. *They decided that these corrupt texts were more accurate because they were the oldest codices currently in existence.* The Westcott-Hort text was created mainly from these two manuscripts despite the massive number of spelling errors in them. This became known as the Alexandrian Text.

Philip Schaff compared each manuscript to the Received Text and stated that in the Gospels alone, the Vaticanus omitted at least 2877 words, added 536, substituted 935, transposed 2098, and modified 1132, for a total of 7578 changes! Schaff also stated that the Sinaiticus omitted 3455 words, added 839, substituted 1114, transposed 2299, and modified 1265; for a total of 8972 changes. Schaff stated the Sinaiticus and Vaticanus were "two of the most corrupt manuscripts in the world.[i]"

Between those two manuscripts there are 3,036 differences between the Sinaiticus and the Vaticanus in the Gospels. Matthew has 656 changes; Mark, 567; Luke, 791; and John, 1022.

---

[i] Philip Schaff, *Companion to the Greek Testament*, London MacMillan, 1833. p119.

Papyri - AD 100 to 300

In this last century over 115 papyri, abbreviated p^1 to p^{115}, have been found in Egypt. These are very ancient fragments of the New Testament ranging from AD 60 to 600. Many people thought these would prove to be entirely the Alexandrian text type, but this was not the case.

The following chart shows which papyri are Alexandrian (missing part of the text), Byzantine (showing the full text), Egyptian-Byzantine (full text rewritten with Egyptian idioms), Western (phrased the way the Latin fathers quoted), Eclectic (mixture of types), and unclassified (fragments too small to tell what family they are from).

---

1 Pure Byzantine papyri - p^{73}

25 Egyptian-Byzantine papyri - p^6, p^8, p^{11}, p^{14}, p^{17}, p^{19}, p^{31}, p^{33}, p^{34}, p^{42}, p^{43}, p^{44}, p^{51}, p^{55}, p^{56}, p^{57}, p^{58}, p^{61}, p^{62}, p^{71}, p^{79}, p^{81}, p^{82}, p^{85}, p^{86}

41 Alexandrian papyri - p^1, p^4, p^5, p^9, p^{10}, p^{12}, p^{13}, p^{15}, p^{16}, p^{18}, p^{20}, p^{22}, p^{23}, p^{24}, p^{26}, p^{27}, p^{28}, p^{29}, p^{30}, p^{32}, p^{35}, p^{39}, p^{40}, p^{46}, p^{47}, p^{49}, p^{52}, p^{53}, p^{64}, p^{65}, p^{67}, p^{70}, p^{72}, p^{74}, p^{75}, p^{78}, p^{80}, p^{87}, p^{90}, p^{104}, p^{115}

15 Eclectic papyri - p^2, p^3, p^{21}, p^{36}, p^{41}, p^{50}, p^{54}, p^{59}, p^{60}, p^{63}, p^{68}, p^{76}, p^{83}, p^{84}, p^{88}

4 Western papyri - p^{37}, p^{38}, p^{45}, p^{48}

30 Unclassified papyri - p^7, p^{25}, p^{66}, p^{69}, p^{77}, p^{79}, p^{89}, p^{91}, p^{92}, p^{93}, p^{94}, p^{95}, p^{96}, p^{97}, p^{98}, p^{99}, p^{100}, p^{101}, p^{102}, p^{103}, p^{105}, p^{106}, p^{107}, p^{108}, p^{109}, p^{110}, p^{111}, p^{112}, p^{113}, p^{114}

Papyri information taken from Wikipedia.com

Out of the 115 papyri, only forty-one are classified as Alexandrian. That is only 36%! The Sinaiticus is western in the first eight chapters of the gospel of John; John 16 and 21 are only *partly* western.

What does this tell us?

No matter how you look at the numbers, the Critical Text and the Received Text existed in the second century AD. Since virtually all the ancient Bibles contain the missing verses and the 86,000 quotes from the church fathers (AD 32-325) quote the missing verses, one should use a Bible based upon the Received Text.

Critical Text

The Critical Text is composed of readings based upon the Sinaiticus and other Alexandrian-type texts. Here are a few of the texts that have been accepted over the years. Remember, Westcott and Hort started with the Sinaiticus and others have corrected their text so that we now have the twenty-seventh edition of the Nestle-Aland Greek Text. Acts is 15% smaller in the Critical Text than in the Received Text. So the Critical Text Bible you read may have more (or less) of the changes.

Lets examine just a few of the altered passages to see how they change doctrine.

Prayer and Fasting

There were several Gnostic cults that repudiated the idea of fasting. It is interesting to note that the CT has eliminated the word "fasting" from *every single* New

Ancient Word of God

Testament passage that mentions prayer and fasting (Matthew 17:21; Mark 9:29; Acts 10:30; and 1 Corinthians 7:5).

Mark 16:9-20
Mark founded the church in Alexandria Egypt, so his gospel was the most widely circulated gospel in Egypt. It makes sense, then, that the Gnostics, who denied Jesus' divinity, would remove the last twelve verses of the last chapter of Mark. This left Christ dead in the tomb, with no resurrection or ascension.

Sun Darkened
In Luke 23:45 the CT changes the text from the sun being darkened to the sun being eclipsed. This is a logical assumption, but this was the 14th of Nisan, during a new moon. An eclipse can only occur on a full moon. This might have been an honest mistake; but it shows an irreverent handling of the Word of God.

Jesus Lied?
In John 7:8 Jesus told his family to go on ahead of Him to the feast because He was "not yet" ready to go. The CT drops the word "yet." I have had many people ask about this passage because it led them to believe Jesus told a lie. He said He would not go up to the feast; then He shows up there anyway! Removing the word "yet" makes Jesus a liar!

See Appendix B for a list of similar problems with the Critical Text.

In light of all this evidence, we should abandon any Bible that is based on the Critical Text and focus solely on the Received Text.

Ancient Word of God

Bibles

Pre-18th Century Bibles

Name	Prepared by	Date
Wycliffe	John Wycliffe	1382
Tyndale New Testament	William Tyndale	1526
Coverdale	Myles Coverdale	1535
Matthew	John Rogers	1537
Great Bible	Myles Coverdale	1537
Taverner	Richard Taverner	1539
Geneva	Protestant/Calvinists	1560
Bishops' Bible	Matthew Parker	1568
Douai-Rheims	Catholics	1582
Authorized King James	Anglicans	1611

These ten Bibles cover a period of 318 years up to AD 1700.

Wycliffe Bible, 1384
John Wycliffe, known as the Morning Star of the Reformation, stated, "The Scriptures are the property of the people and no one should be allowed to wrest it from them." The first Wycliffe Bible was a literal translation from the Latin Vulgate. Purvey revised it in 1395. In 1415 the Council of Constance ordered all Wycliffe Bibles to be burned and Wycliffe's bones dug up and burned. This was done in 1428.

The Tyndale Bible, 1525
William Tyndale produced the first printed Scriptures in English. To a high religious leader of his time he stated,

> "If God spare my life, ere many years I will cause a boy that driveth the plow shall know more of the Scripture than thou dost."

After trying to gain support in London for about a year, Tyndale went to Germany where Luther was translating the Scriptures into German. Skilled in seven languages, Tyndale used what manuscripts he had in Greek and Hebrew to translate into English. Of the first 3,000 books shipped to England, only a portion of one still exists. It is said that nine-tenths of the Authorized Version is still Tyndale. Tyndale was burned at the stake in 1535 for trying to give the Scriptures to the people.

The Coverdale Bible, 1535
Myles Coverdale was the first to print the complete Bible in English. He followed the example of Martin Luther by placing the Apocrypha in the center of the Bible. He also added 1st and 2nd Esdras but omitted the prayer of Manasseh. His Old Testament version was based on German Bibles and the Latin Vulgate.

Matthew's Bible, 1537
Matthew's Bible is the work of John Rogers. He combined the Tyndale and Coverdale Bibles into Matthew's Bible, putting the prayer of Manasseh back in. He was the first martyr to be burned at the stake by Queen Mary in her efforts to rid England of any traces of the Reformation. This Bible was translated into English from at least five different languages, including French.

The Great Bible, 1539
Many groups disliked the marginal notes in both Matthew's Bible and Coverdale's Bible. King Henry VIII set Myles Coverdale to work on this Bible which would be free from any interpretation. This was the first version to have part of the Apocrypha translated from the Greek. After two years of debate, in 1541, it was placed in the churches. It was the first "authorized version." Much of

the Old Testament was translated from German and the Latin Vulgate.

The Geneva Bible, 1560
Geneva, Switzerland, was a neutral city and home to John Calvin and Theodore Beza. The Geneva Bible became the most-loved Bible among Protestants until it was finally replaced in popularity by the King James Version (KJV) in 1644. The thousands of Calvinistic notes contained in this version inflamed the Church of England and the Church of Rome, alike. The Old Testament in this version is based on the Hebrew Old Testament.

The Bishops' Bible, 1568
After seeing the popularity of the Geneva Bible grow, the Archbishop of Canterbury, Matthew Parker, led a group of Anglican Bishops to translate the Bible. It was uneven in quality; but by 1602 it had become the second "authorized version." Most of the Old Testament was translated from the Hebrew. Other parts of the Old Testament and the Apocrypha came from the Latin Vulgate.

The Douai-Rheims Bible, 1608
The Douai-Rheims was a Catholic version with anti-Protestant notes meant to counter the Geneva Bible. It is based on the Latin Vulgate.

The King James Version, 1611
King James VI was king of Scotland for thirty-six years. He succeeded Queen Elizabeth I in 1603 and became King James of England. While the Great Bible and the Bishops' Bible were the authorized versions, the masses were using the Geneva Bible. King James ordered "the best-learned from both universities," to make a neutral translation of the Bible without notes, neither Calvinistic

nor Catholic, to be used instead of the Douai-Rheims and the Geneva, "and so the whole church to be bound unto it, and none other." It became the best loved Bible of the English language. Fifty-four of the best Protestant and Catholic scholars were chosen on June 30, 1604; but only forty-seven names appear on the list of those who actually did the work. The translation was based on Greek and Hebrew, not on Latin.

There were several minor editions of the KJV Bible printed to clear up various misspellings. The last edition was completed in 1769, which is still the edition we use today. Only the KJV continued to be updated for modern English.

Here are a few examples of the archaic English for these early versions.

"And God seide, Liȝt be maad; and liȝt was maad." *Genesis 1:3 Wycliffe*

"And God said, Let there be light: and there was light." *Genesis 1:3 KJV*

"This is the boke of the generacion of Iesus Christ the sonne of Dauid the sonne also of Abraham." *Matthew 1:1 Tyndale*

"The book of the generacioun of Jhesu Crist, the sone of Dauid, the sone of Abraham." *Matthew 1:1 Wycliffe*

"This is the booke of the generation of Iesus Christ, the sonne of Dauid, the sonne of Abraham." *Matthew 1:1 Bishops'*

"The booke of the generation of Iesvs Christ the sonne of Dauid, the sonne of Abraham."
Matthew 1:1 Geneva

"This is the boke of the generacion of Iesus Christ ye sonne of Dauid, the sonne of Abraham."
Matthew 1:1 Coverdale

"The booke of the generation of Iesus Christ, the sonne of Dauid, the sonne of Abraham."
Matthew 1:1 KJV 1611

Conclusion

Of these ten Bibles, only the Geneva and King James Bibles were translated from the Hebrew Old Testament. We could use either of these two Bibles as a guide for accuracy; but of these two, only the King James continued to be updated into modern English.

18th and 19th Century Bibles

Abbreviation	Title	Date
Mace	Mace New Testament	1729
Whiston	Whiston's Primitive New Testament	1745
Challoner	Richard Challoner	1752
	Wesley New Testament	1755
Quaker	Anthony Purver	1764
	Thomson's Translation	1808
JST	Joseph Smith's Translation	1830
Webster	Webster's Revision - Noah Webster	1833
LONT	Living Oracles New Testament	1835
Etheridge	Etheridge's Peshitta	1849
Murdock	Murdock's Peshitta	1852
	Leeser Bible	1853
YLT	Young's Literal Translation- Robert Young	1862
	Emphatic Diaglott	1864
Anderson	Anderson's 1865 New Testament	1865
Noyes	New Testament	1869
Julia	Julia E. Smith Parker Translation	1876
RV	Revised Version	1885
DBY	Darby Bible - John Nelson Darby	1890

These nineteen Bibles cover a period of 200 years.

Mace New Testament, 1729

Mace created a thought-for-thought translation of the New Testament. He based most of this research on Unitarian John Mill's *Greek New Testament*.

Whiston's Primitive New Testament, 1745

William Whiston was a non-trinitarian. He is famous for this New Testament and his translation of Josephus.

Challoner Bible, 1752

Challoner revised the Douai-Rheims Bible. Douai-Rheims is the Catholic Bible based on the Latin Vulgate with anti-Protestant notes.

Wesley New Testament, 1755

John Wesley wrote his New Testament, consisting of the KJV with very few changes and a series of explanatory notes. The notes are still available, detached from the translation.

Quaker Bible, 1764

Anthony Purver, a Quaker, created his own version of the Bible. Very little is known about this extremely rare Bible.

Thomson's Translation, 1808

This is Charles Thomson's Translation of the Septuagint Old Testament.

Joseph Smith's Translation, 1830

Joseph Smith, founder of the Mormon cult, started his own translation of the Bible in 1830, but he never finished it.

Webster's Revision, 1833

Noah Webster's Bible replaced some archaic words like "why" for "wherefore" and "lewd woman" for "whore." Over all, it changed very little from the KJV it is based upon.

Living Oracles New Testament, 1835

This New Testament was created by Alexander Campbell. It is a modified KJV with passages removed to align it to the Critical Text. His Bibles were burned and he was almost burned at the stake for this translation.

Etheridge's Translation of the Peshitta, 1849

This New Testament was translated from the Syriac.

Murdock 's Translation of the Peshitta, 1852

This New Testament was also translated from the Syriac.

Leeser Bible, 1853

This Bible was the first Jewish Old Testament produced in English.

Young's Literal Translation, 1862

Robert Young produced this literal, word-for-word translation of the Bible in 1862, revising it a year before his death in 1887. Young was a member of the Free Church in England.

Emphatic Diaglott, 1864

This Greek New Testament was produced by a Christadelphian named Benjamin Wilson, *who had no Greek credentials*. Wilson denied the personal pre-existence of Christ, and the entire incarnation doctrine. Wilson was anti-trinitarian. This version is used widely by Jehovah's Witnesses because of its anti-trinitarian bias. It has added the article "a," (not found in the Greek text) to read "a god" for John 1:1, like the Jehovah's Witnesses New World Translation (NWT).

New Testament, 1869
This Unitarian work was created by George R. Noyes.

Julia E. Smith Parker Translation, 1876
Julia Parker was self taught in Hebrew, but this rare Bible is said to be a very literal word-for-word translation. Her odd way of translating the Hebrew, using the Hebrew imperfect tense with the English future tense, made her translation very mechanical and nonsensical.

Revised Version, 1885
The Revised Version (also known as the English Revised Version) was the only authorized revision of the KJV 1611. It was created by more than fifty scholars from various denominations from England. The New Testament was published in 1881, the Old Testament in 1885, and the Apocrypha in 1895. Two of the leading translators were Brooke Foss Westcott and Fenton John Anthony Hort.

Darby Bible, 1890
John Nelson Darby authored the Darby Bible. Darby is called the father of modern dispensationalism. He taught a pretribulation Rapture and the return of the state of Israel according to Bible prophecy.

18th and 19th Century Bibles

20th Century Bibles

Abbrev.	Title	Date
ASV	American Standard Version	1901
EBR	Rotherham's Emphasized Bible	1902
TCNT	The Twentieth Century New Testament	1902
Godbey	Godbey New Testament	1902
Fenton	The Holy Bible in Modern English	1903
WNT	Weymouth New Testament	1903
WAS	Worrell New Testament	1904
WVSS	Westminster Version of the Sacred Scriptures	1913
JPS	Jewish Publication Society of America Version	1917
RNT	Riverside New Testament	1923
MRB	Modern Reader's Bible	
CTNT	Centenary New Testament	1924
MNT	James Moffatt Bible	1926
Lamsa	Lamsa Bible	1933
AAT	An American Translation	1935
Greber	The New Testament	1937
WmNT	Williams New Testament	1937
SPC	Spencer New Testament	1941
CCD	Confraternity Bible	1941
BBE	Bible in Basic English	1949
NWT	New World Translation	1950
RSV	Revised Standard Version	1952
Knox	Knox Translation of the Vulgate	1955
TANT	The Authentic New Testament	1955
HSM	Holy Scriptures Masoretic Text	1955
KLNT	Kleist-Lilly New Testament	1956
PME	Phillips New Testament in Modern English	1958
BV	The Berkeley Version	1958
CKJV	Children's King James Version	1960
WET	Wuest Expanded Translation	1961
NSNT	Norlie's Simplified New Testament	1961
TDB	The Dartmouth Bible	1961
NNT	Noli New Testament	1961
CKJB	Children's King James Bible	1962
HNB	Holy Name Bible	1963
AMP	Amplified Bible	1965

Knoch	Concordant Literal Version	1966
JB	Jerusalem Bible	1966
RSV-CE	Revised Standard Version Catholic Edition	1966
BNT	The New Testament: A New Translation	1968
	Cotton Patch Bible	1968
BWE	Bible in Worldwide English (NT)	1969
MLB	Modern Language Bible	1969
TBR	The Bible Reader	1969
NEB	New English Bible	1970
NAB	New American Bible	1970
KJII	King James II	1971
KJV20	King James Version – Twentieth Century Edition	
TLB	The Living Bible	1971
TSB	The Story Bible	1971
TLB-CE	The Living Bible Catholic Edition	1971
NASB	New American Standard Bible	1971 1995
LivEng	The Bible In Living English	1972
SNB	Restoration of Original Sacred Name Bible	1976
BECK	An American Translation	1976
GNB	Good News Bible	1976 1992
IB	Interlinear Bible (Green)	1976
NIV	New International Version	1978
SEB	Simple English Bible	1980
SSBE	Sacred Scriptures Bethel Edition	1981
NKJV	New King James Version	1982
	A New Accurate Translation	1984
NJB	New Jerusalem Bible	1985
NJPS	New Jewish Publication Society of America Version	1985
LITV	Green's Literal Translation	1985
ONT	Original New Testament	1985
KIT	Kingdom Interlinear Translation	1985
CCB	Christian Community Bible	1986
NLV	New Life Version	1986
MCT	McCord's New Testament	1988
NRSV	New Revised Standard Version	1989
NRSV-CE	New Revised Standard Version Catholic Edition	1989
JNT	Jewish New Testament	1989
REB	Revised English Bible	1989

ERV	Easy-to-Read Version	1989
GNC	God's New Covenant (NT)	1989
EVD	English Version for the Deaf	1989
KJ21	21st Century King James	1991
NCV	New Century Version	1991
Gaus	Unvarnished New Testament	1991
TEV	Today's English Version	1992
	Clear Word	1994
GW	God's Word	1995
CEV	Contemporary English Version	1995
AST	Anointed Standard Version	1995
AIV	An Inclusive Version	1995
NIrV	New International Reader's Version	1996
NIVI	New International Inclusive Language	1996
	The New Testament (Lattimore)	1996
NLT	New Living Translation	1996 2004
TMB	Third Millennium Bible	1998
CJB	Complete Jewish Bible	1998
TS98	The Scriptures '98 Version	1998
RcV	Recovery Version	1999
MKJV	Modern King James Version	1999
AKJV	American King James Version	1999
TCE	The Common Edition New Testament	1999
ALT	Analytical-Literal Translation	1999
	The Last Days New Testament	1999

These ninety-eight Bibles cover a period of 100 years.

American Standard Version, 1901
In reaction to the English Revised Version, American scholars created the American Standard Version based on the KJV and the corrupt manuscripts.

Rotherham's Emphasized Bible, 1902
Created by J. B. Rotherham, this Bible was based on the work by Westcott and Hort.

The Twentieth Century New Testament, 1902
This New Testament was based on the debased Westcott and Hort text.

Godbey New Testament, 1902
This New Testament was published by preterist (non-premillennialist) Dr. W.B. Godbey.

Ferrar Fenton Bible, 1903
This text is now quite rare. Fenton believed in British Israelism.[j] Because of this, it was a favorite Bible of white supremacists groups for a number of years.

Weymouth New Testament, 1903
Richard Francis Weymouth created this English New Testament from what he said was his own Greek Text. His Greek text was partly based on Westcott and Hort.

Worrell New Testament, 1904
This New Treatment was translated by A. S. Worrell, based on the Westcott-Hort Greek Text.

Westminster Version of the Sacred Scriptures, 1913
This was an unofficial Catholic New Testament and partial Old Testament published in 1913. It was replaced by the Confraternity Bible in 1944.

Jewish Publication Society Old Testament (JPS OT)
This Old Testament was published in 1917.

---

[j] A cultic belief that the English are the true Jewish people.

Ancient Word of God

Riverside New Testament, 1923
This Bible follows the tradition of the Twentieth Century New Testament, Weymouth, Moffat, and the Revised Version. It was written in paragraph form without numbering of verses.

Modern Reader's Bible, 1923
This Bible was based on the Revised Version and edited by Richard G. Moulton.

Centenary Translation of the New Testament, 1924
This New Testament was translated by Helen Barrett Montgomery. It was reprinted in 1988 under the title *The New Testament in Modern English*, with a spine and cover labeled *Montgomery New Testament*. It was based partly on Weymouth's 1903 translation.

Moffatt Bible, 1926
This Bible, translated by James Mofatt, was based on the corrupted Greek text by Hermann Freiherr von Soden, called the Majority Text (MT).

Lamsa Bible, 1933
Dr. George Lamsa translated this Bible from the Aramaic Peshitta, not the Greek text.

An American Translation, 1935
This Bible was produced by combining the New Testament of Edgar J. Goodspeed and Smith's Old Testament.

The New Testament: A New Translation based on the Oldest Manuscripts by Johannes Greber, 1937

Johannes Greber, a Catholic turned spiritist, translated this version of the New Testament with the help of spirit guides. It was reprinted for a short time in 1980. Jehovah's Witnesses cite this translation frequently. Like the New World Translation, it had "the word was a god" in John 1:1.

Williams New Testament, 1937

This New Testament was created by Charles B. Williams.

Spencer New Testament, 1941

Francis Aloysius Spencer published this Catholic translation of the New Testament from the Latin Vulgate.

Confraternity Bible, 1941

This Catholic Bible is a revision of the Challoner revision of the Douai-Rheims Bible based on the Latin Vulgate.

Bible in Basic English, 1949

This Bible was translated by Professor S. H. Hooke using the standard 850 Basic English words.

New World Translation, 1950

This Bible was produced by the Jehovah's Witness cult. It is well known for its deliberate changing of Scripture passages to obscure the deity of Jesus Christ.

Ancient Word of God

Revised Standard Version, 1952
This Bible was an attempt to update the American Standard Version of 1901.

Knox Bible, 1955
Ronald Knox produced this Catholic Bible based on the Latin Vulgate.

The Authentic New Testament, 1955
Hugh J. Schonfield, a Jewish author, produced this New Testament. This is the same man who authored the famous book, *The Passover Plot*. He believed Jesus was just a man who tried to become a messiah. Some of the changes in this New Testament include "immersion" instead of "baptism," "community" instead of "church," "envoy" instead of "apostle," "supervisor" instead of "bishop," and "administrator" instead of "deacon."

Holy Scriptures of the Masoretic Text, 1955
This Old Testament was a remake of the Jewish Publication Society's Old Testament.

Kleist-Lilly New Testament, 1956
This was a new Catholic version produced by James A. Kleist. It seems to add too many new phrases to clear up the text. Example: "When time began, the Word was there, and the Word was face to face with God, and the Word was God."

Phillips New Testament in Modern English, 1958

This Bible was translated by Anglican clergyman J. B. Phillips. The most famous passage from this translation is a portion of Romans 12:2, "Don't let the world around you squeeze you into its own mould."

Berkeley Version, 1959

Gerrit Verkuyl was the editor for this version. It was later revised as the Modern Language Bible of 1969.

Children's King James Version, 1960

J. P. Green created this version of the King James Bible for children.

The Dartmouth Bible, 1961

This version of the KJV has been rewritten with books placed in a different order and with several books combined. About one half of the original content has been lost.

The Simplified New Testament, 1961

This Bible was translated by Olaf M. Norlie.

Noli New Testament, 1961

This 1961 New Testament is an English translation of the Greek text used by the Greek Orthodox Church.

Wuest Expanded Translation, 1961

This Bible was translated by Kenneth S. Wuest, who was a professor of New Testament Greek at Moody Bible Institute in Chicago, until his death in 1962.

Holy Name Bible, 1963
This Bible is a reworking of the KJV by Angelo B. Traina, a minister with the Church of God, Seventh Day. It replaced the phrase, "the cross," with "torture stake." The Church of God, Seventh Day was founded in 1863. They hold to annihilationism[k], worship on Saturday, and they also reject the doctrine of the Trinity.

Amplified Bible, 1965
This Bible added synonyms for important words in each verse. This was based on English, however, and not Greek.

Concordant Literal Version, 1966
This Bible is based on the Westcott and Hort Greek.

Jerusalem Bible, 1966
This Bible is a Catholic version translated from the Greek and Hebrew instead of the Vulgate. It has a 72-week prophecy instead of a 70-week prophecy in Daniel 9.

Revised Standard Version, Catholic Edition, 1966
This is a Catholic version of the RSV.

The New Testament: A New Translation, 1968
This Bible was translated by William Barclay. Barclay was a Universalist[l] who denied the divinity of Jesus.

---

[k] Annihilationism is the doctrine that there is no eternal Hell. It says that people who are cast into Hell are completely destroyed and cease to exist.

[l] Universalism is the belief that everyone will eventually be saved.

The Bible Reader, 1968

This Bible was a product of a joint Catholic and Protestant committee and contains the Apocrypha. It was prepared by Walter M. Abbott, S. J.; Rabbi Arthur Gilbert; Rolfe Lanier Hunt; and J. Carter Swaim.

Bible in Worldwide English (NT), 1969

This paraphrase used simplified English designed for those who speak English as a second language, originally written by Annie Cressman.

Modern Language Bible, 1969

This Bible began as the work of Gerrit Verkuyl, a minister of the Presbyterian Church USA.

New English Bible, 1970

This Bible was printed with the Apocrypha.

New American Bible, 1970

This Catholic Bible replaced the 1941 Confraternity Bible.

King James II, 1971

This Bible was translated by J. P. Green, a member of the Presbyterian Church in America.

King James Version – Twentieth Century Edition

This is an update to the KJV by J. P. Green. It is out of print.

The Living Bible, 1971

This Bible is a paraphrase, not recommended for study.

Ancient Word of God

The Story Bible, 1971
This Bible is another paraphrase.

The Living Bible, Catholic Edition, 1971
This Bible is the Catholic edition of the Living Bible.

New American Standard Bible, 1971
This Bible was an update of the American Standard Version of 1901. It was updated again in 1995.

The Bible in Living English, 1972
This Bible was translated by Steven T. Byington and was published by the Watchtower Bible and Tract Society (the Jehovah's Witnesses).

Restoration of Original Sacred Name Bible, 1976
This Bible is a revision of the Rotherham Version using the Hebrew names for God and Jesus, Yahweh and Yeshua.

An American Translation, 1976
This Bible was published at the Lutheran Church-Missouri Synod's Concordia Publishing House.

Good News Bible, 1976
This Bible was also called Today's English Version (TEV).

Interlinear Bible, 1976
This Bible was created by J. P. Green. It contains the Literal Version (also written by him), based on the Received Text. It also contains the Greek and Hebrew in

interlinear^m form. This is a very good translation of the Received Text.

New International Version, 1978
The NIV was the first Critical Text Bible to replace the KJV in popularity. The NIV had more missing verses than any other translation up to its time.

Simple English Bible, 1980
This Bible was based on a limited 3000-word vocabulary and every day sentence structure. It was also marketed as the Plain English Bible, the International English Bible, and the God Chasers Extreme New Testament.

Sacred Scriptures Bethel Edition, 1981
This Bible was created by the Assemblies of Yahweh, a messianic cult that rejects the doctrine of the trinity.

New King James Version, 1982
This Bible is a new translation of the KJV based on the Received Text.

A New Accurate Translation, 1984
This New Testament was created by Julian G. Anderson, a Lutheran pastor. The books are arranged in their presumed chronological order.

---

^m An Interlinear is a Bible with the Greek/Hebrew on one line with the English under it. Usually it has a third line with Strong's numbers to make Greek/Hebrew studies easier.

New Jerusalem Bible, 1985
This is a Catholic update to the 1966 Jerusalem Bible.

New Jewish Publication Society of America Version
This 1985 Old Testament is a revision of the 1917 version.

Green's Literal Translation, 1985
This Bible was translated by J. P. Green based on the Received Text.

Original New Testament, 1985
This Bible is a rerelease of Hugh J. Schonfield's New Testament. This is the same author of the famous book, *The Passover Plot*. He believed Jesus was just a man who tried to become a messiah.

Christian Community Bible, 1986
This Bible was created by liberal Roman Catholics in the Philippines. The notes teach things such as the Genesis creation account is simply pagan folklore.

New Life Version, 1986
This Bible was designed for people who speak English as a second language. It uses a limited vocabulary of only 850 words.

McCord's New Testament, 1988
This Bible was written by Hugo McCord (1911-2004) of the Churches of Christ in America. It was also known as

the *Everlasting Gospel*, and the *Freed-Hardeman Version*.

New Revised Standard Version 1989
This Bible is a revision of the 1952 Revised Standard Version.

Jewish New Testament 1989
This Bible is David H. Stern's Messianic New Testament.

Revised English Bible 1989
This Bible is a revision of the New English Bible of 1970.

Easy-to-Read Version 1989
This Bible is another simplified English translation.

God's New Covenant, 1989
The New Testament was written by H. W. Cassirer.

English Version for the Deaf, 1989
This version is an over-simplified version, confusing many passages.

21st Century King James, 1991
This Bible is a revision of the KJV 1611 by Deuel Enterprises.

New Century Version, 1991
This Bible is a revision of the International Children's Bible (ICB). This Bible elevated its reading level from third grade to fifth. It is a gender-neutral translation.

Unvarnished New Testament, 1991
This Bible was translated by Andy Gaus. It is another attempt at a very simplified Bible. It replaces words like "sin" with the phrase "doing wrong."

Clear Word, 1994
This Bible is a Seventh Day Adventist paraphrase.

God's Word, 1995
This Bible was translated by the God's Word to the Nations Society.

Contemporary English Version, 1995
This Bible was published by the American Bible Society.

Anointed Standard Version, 1995
This Bible was written by V. S. Herrell and is used by white supremacist groups like the Arian Nations.

An Inclusive Version, 1995
This feminist Bible refers to God as the Father-Mother; Jesus is not the Son of God but the Child of the Divine.

New International Reader's Version, 1996
This Bible is a simplification of the New International Version for young readers.

New International Version Inclusive Language Edition
This 1996 Bible was a gender-inclusive version of the NIV. In 1997, an article by World Magazine accused the

NIVI of being "a feminist seduction of the evangelical church."

The New Testament (Lattimore), 1996
This Bible was translated by Richmond A. Lattimore by very closely following the Westcott and Hort text.

New Living Translation, 1996
This Bible, updated in 2004, was a fresh translation based on the style of the Living Bible paraphrase of 1971.

Third Millennium Bible, 1998
This Bible is a reworked KJV 1611 including the Apocrypha with minor changes. It was also published as the NAV, New Authorized Version.

Complete Jewish Bible, 1998
This Bible was created by Dr. David H. Stern. The Old Testament is a paraphrase of the 1917 Jewish Publication Society version of the Tanakh. The New Testament is his own translation called the Jewish New Testament (JNT).

The Scriptures '98 Version, 1998
This Bible was published by the Institute for Scripture Research (ISR). This group refuses to give their doctrinal position on any subject and will not respond to inquiry as to their qualifications.

Recovery Version, 1999
This Bible was produced by the Local Church, a non-Trinitarian cult.

Ancient Word of God

Modern King James Version, 1999
This Bible was produced by J. P. Green based on the Received Text.

American King James Version, 1999
This Bible was placed in public domain by Michael Peter (Stone) Engelbrite.

The Common Edition New Testament, 1999
This New Testament was edited by T.E. Clontz and was designed to be a simplified Bible for easy reading.

Analytical-Literal Translation, 1999
This New Testament was created by Gary F. Zeolla

The Last Days New Testament, 1999
This New Testament was created by Ray W. Johnson for the purpose of teaching a post-tribulation Rapture.

21st Century Bibles

Abbreviation	Title	Date
UKJV	Updated King James Version	2000
KJV2000	King James 2000 Version	2000
SSFOY	Sacred Scriptures, Family of Yah Edition	2000
RKJNT	Revised King James New Testament	2000
EEB	Easy English Bible	2001
KJVER	King James Version Easy Reading	2001
ESV	English Standard Version	2001
HSV	Holy Scriptures Version	2001
	2001 Translation	2001
UTV	Urim Thummim Version	2001
WV	Wycliffe Version (Noble)	2001
MSG	The Message	2002
OJB	Orthodox Jewish Bible	2002
	A Fresh Parenthetical Translation (NT)	2002
HNC	Holy New Covenant	2002
TWOY	The Word of Yahweh	2003
CKJV	Comfort-able King James Version	2003
EMTV	English Majority Text Version	2003
ABP	Apostolic Bible Polyglot	2003
FNT	Faithful New Testament	2003
VW	A Voice in the Wilderness Holy Scriptures	2003
CGV	Context Group Version	2003
HCSB	Holman Christian Standard Bible	2004
AB	Apostles' Bible	2004
HRV	Hebraic-Roots Version	2004
TSNT	The Source New Testament	2004
Younan	Younan's Peshitta Interlinear	2004
NSB	New Simplified Bible	2004
TNIV	Today's New international Version	2005
NET	New English Translation	2005
NCPB	New Cambridge Paragraph Bible	2005
SN-KJ	Sacred Name King James Bible	2005
KJ3	KJ3—Literal Translation Bible	2005
CAB	Complete Apostles Bible	2005
ACV	A Conservative Version	2005
	Renovaré Spiritual Formation Bible	2005

	Life with God Study Bible	2005
WNT	William's New Testament	2005
UVNT	Understandable Version New Testament	2005
Chb	Christolog Bible	2005
ARTB	Ancient Roots Translinear Bible	2006
AV7	AV7 (New Authorized Version)	2006
AVU	Authorized Version Update	2006
	Spirit of Prophecy Study Bible	2006
NETS	New English Translation of the Septuagint	2007
OSB	Orthodox Study Bible	2007
ICB	International Children's Bible	2007
NIBEV	Natural Israelite Bible, English Version	2007
TB	The Besorah (plagiarized '98 version)	2008
COM	The Comprehensive New Testament	2008
	The Voice	2008
NHEB	New Heart English Bible	2008
HOB	Holy Orthodox Bible	2008
TNB	Tarish Nephite Bible	2008
ANT	Accurate New Testament	2008
CPDV	Catholic Public Domain Version	2009
UPDV	Updated Version	2009
WGCIB	The Work of God's Children Illustrated Bible	2010
OEB	Open English Bible	2010
NIV10	NIV 2010	2010
LEB	Lexham English Bible	2010
EOB	Eastern / Greek Orthodox Bible	2010
NABRE	New American Bible Revised Edition	2011
MLV	Modern Literal Version New Testament	2011
EB	Expanded Bible	2011
TrLB	Tree of Life Bible	2011
WEB	World English Bible	-
WEB-ME	World English Bible, Messianic Edition	-
HNV	Hebrew Names Version	-
CBP	Conservative Bible Project	-
DRP	David Robert Palmer Translation	-
RNKJV	Restored Name King James Version	-
MGB	The Manga Bible	-
ISV	International Standard Version	-
Jubilee2000	English Jubilee 2000 Bible	-
YLR	Young's Literal Revised	-

FAA	Far Above All New Testament	-
Szasz	Awful New Testament (Emery Szasz)	-
MASV	Modern American Standard Version	-
TEB	Transparent English Bible	-
TFB	The Free Bible	-
DB	Disciples' Bible	-
	Victorious Gospel of Jesus Christ New Covenant Translation	-

- Internet based or not yet published

These eighty-three Bibles cover a period of just eleven years.

Updated King James Version, 2000
This Bible is a KJV with updated spellings and archaic words replaced.

KJV2000, 2000
This is an update to the KJV by a Baptist, Robert A. Couric.

Sacred Scriptures, Family of Yah Edition, 2000
This is a non-KJV sacred name version, using words like Yahweh for God and Yeshua for Jesus.

Revised King James New Testament, 2000
Brad Haugaard revised the KJV by removing verses to match the modern English editions.

Easy English Bible, 2001
Wycliffe Associates (UK) developed Easy English for non-English speakers.

King James Version Easy Reading, 2001
This Bible is the King James 1611 with minor word changes, which are listed in the front of the Bible. Both the Old Testament and New Testament print out the words of God in red.

English Standard Version, 2001
The ESV is a revision of the 1971 edition of the Revised Standard Version. It has been adopted as the official Bible of the Reformed Churches of America.

Holy Scriptures Version, 2001
This Bible was created by Vincent Rabon Jr. It is based on the KJV, but has received some criticism because the translator doesn't speak any of the original languages of the Bible, and made his translations using a computer program. There is also some criticism that there is a denominational bias towards Church of Christ teachings.

2001 Translation
This Bible's Old Testament is based on the Septuagint and its New Testament is based on the Aramaic.

Urim Thummim Version, 2001
This translation, written by Dallas Everette James, adds the book of Enoch to the canon of Scriptures.

Wycliffe Version (Noble), 2001
Terence Noble translated this modern spelling version of the Wycliffe Bible.

The Message, 2002
This is a paraphrase, not recommended for study.

Orthodox Jewish Bible, 2002
This is Phillip Goble's Messianic Bible. It contains a lot of Yinglish (Yiddish and English vocabulary).

A Fresh Parenthetical Translation, 2002
This New Testament is more of a paraphrase similar to the Message, than a translation. It was developed by Methodist layperson B. E. Junkins.

Holy New Covenant
The Galilee Translation Project created this New Testament. This version is missing verses.

The Word of Yahweh, 2003
This Bible is produced by the Assemblies of Yahweh, a messianic nontrinitarian cult in Bethel, Pennsylvania.

Comfort-able King James Version, 2003
This Bible was a KJV that was used as the basis for the Evidence Bible. The difference between the KJV and the Comfort-able KJV was so slight that the Comfort-able KJV was discontinued and the Evidence Bible now uses the regular KJV.

English Majority Text Version, 2003
This New Testament by Paul Esposito is based on a new Majority Text.

Apostolic Bible Polyglot, 2003
This Bible's Old Testament is based on the Septuagint. A polyglot is a book written in multiple languages.

Faithful New Testament, 2003
This New Testament was written by William Wilde Zeitler.

A Voice in the Wilderness Holy Scriptures, 2003
This Bible was written by Paul Becker, based on the Masoretic Text and the Textus Receptus, or Received Text.

Context Group Version, 2003
This Bible is based on the conclusions of the Jesus Seminar. The sayings of Jesus are divided into groups of what they have decided Jesus said, what He might have said, and what He did not say.

Holman Christian Standard Bible, 2004
This Bible started out as a Majority Text translation but the death of the editor halfway through the project resulted in it being another Critical Text version.

Apostles' Bible, 2004
This Bible is a fresh translation of the Septuagint and the majority text by Paul W. Esposito.

Hebraic Roots Version, 2004
This Bible was created by nontrinitarian James Trimm.

The Source New Testament, 2004
This Bible is gender inclusive and targeted toward gays and lesbians.

Younan's Peshitta Interlinear, 2004
This is the first interlinear Bible based on the Aramaic Peshitta.

New Simplified Bible, 2004
This Bible was created by nontrinitarian James R. Madsen.

Today's New International Version, 2005
This is an update of the 1978 New International Version. In addition to the missing verses of its predecessor it was created to be gender neutral. There was such an outrage over this that this version was discontinued.

New English Translation, 2005
The NET Bible was developed online as a new translation, not an update of any older version. It has cut out several Bible verses.

New Cambridge Paragraph Bible, 2005
This Bible is a KJV with modernized spelling. It was based on the KJV1611 and Bishops' Bibles and contains the Apocrypha. It is written in paragraph form for literary style. The most striking point of interest is that it also eliminates the "supplied words" usually printed in italics in current KJVs.

Sacred Name King James Bible, 2005
John Hurt produced this KJV with messianic names for God and Jesus and a few other changes.

KJ3—Literal Translation Bible, 2005
This Bible, produced by J. P. Green, is a word-for-word translation of the Received Test. It uses Jehovah in place of the Lord.

Complete Apostles Bible, 2005
This Bible is a fresh translation of the Septuagint and the Majority Text by Paul W. Esposito.

A Conservative Version, 2005
Walter L. Porter (a professor at a Churches of Christ University) produced this Bible.

Renovaré Spiritual Formation Bible, 2005
This is an Emergent[n] Bible. The lead editor is Richard J. Foster.

Life with God Bible, 2005
This is another Emergent[o] Bible with lead editor, Richard J. Foster.

William's New Testament, 2005
This New Testament was written by Charles B. Williams.

---

[n] The Emergent movement is a movement that has added Roman Catholic idols and contemplative prayer (Biblical sorcery) to their rituals.
[o] Ibid.

Understandable Version New Testament, 2005
William E. Paul, a Church of Christ pastor, produced this New Testament with notes bracketed in the text rather than in footnote form.

Christolog Bible, 2005
This is a "corrected" KJV by R. P. Carroll. Among its many corrections, it cut out several of the more important verses.

Ancient Roots Translinear Bible, 2006
This Hebrew/Aramaic interlinear was created by Ms. A. Frances Werner.

AV7, 2006
This Bible is a KJV edited by a computer program modernizing the text.

Authorized Version Update, 2006
This Bible is a KJV update by Leland M. Haines.

Spirit of Prophecy Study Bible, 2006
This Bible is a Seventh Day Adventist Bible.

New English Translation of the Septuagint, 2007
This Old Testament is a new English translation of the Septuagint.

Orthodox Study Bible, 2007
This Bible, put together by Eastern Orthodox scholars, is based on the Septuagint.

International Children's Bible, 2007
This children's book contains stories adapted from the Contemporary English Version.

Natural Israelite Bible, English Version, 2007
This Bible is another sacred name KJV.

The Besorah, 2008
This is a plagiarized remake of the Scriptures '98 Version.

The Comprehensive New Testament, 2008
This New Testament has each New Testament verse listing parallels from the Apocrypha, Dead Sea Scrolls, Dhammapada, Egyptian Book of the Dead, Josephus, Nag Hammadi Library, New Testament Apocrypha, Old Testament, Patristic Fathers, Philo, Plato, Pseudepigrapha, Pythagoras, Tacitus, and the Talmud!

The Voice, 2008
This is an Emergent[p] paraphrase of the New Testament.

New Heart English Bible, 2008
This version is based on the American Standard Version first published in 1901.

Holy Orthodox Bible, 2008
This Bible is a Greek Orthodox Bible written by Peter Papoutsis.

---

[p] The Emergent movement is a movement that has added Roman Catholic idols and contemplative prayer (Biblical sorcery) to their rituals.

Tarish Nephite Bible, 2008
This Bible is the official Bible of the Nephite Church of Christ (Mormon offshoot).

Accurate New Testament, 2008
This New Testament was based on the Alexandrian Text.

Catholic Public Domain Version, 2009
This is a Roman Catholic online version produced to be free.

Updated Version, 2009
This version includs the Apocrypha. It also takes out the virgin birth in Luke 1 by saying Mary was the wife of Joseph who could not have children!

The Work of God's Children Illustrated Bible, 2010
This Catholic version is based on the Douay-Rheims Bible Challoner Revision.

Open English Bible, 2010
This is a revision of the 1902 The Twentieth Century New Testament based on the Westcott and Hort text.

NIV, 2010
This is the current update for the 1978 New International Version.

Ancient Word of God

Lexham English Bible, 2010
Logos software produced this as a standard New Testament and as an Interlinear. Its chief editor was W. Hall Harris, III.

Eastern / Greek Orthodox Bible, 2010
This is another Greek Orthodox Translation with a Septuagint Old Testament.

The New American Bible Revised Edition, 2011
This is the current Roman Catholic Bible.

Modern Literal Version, 2011
This Bible was written by G. Allen Walker.

Expanded Bible, 2011
This is a Calvinist Bible.

Tree of Life Bible, 2011
This is another Messianic Bible.

The Following are either internet-only Bibles or Bibles that have been published on the internet for free, but have no printed editions available, yet.

World English Bible
This is a modern update to the 1901 American Standard Version. It is available free on the web and is without

copyright. It contains the Old and New Testaments and the Apocrypha.

World English Bible Messianic Edition
This Bible is a sacred name remake of the World English Bible, and is known as the Hebrew Names Version (HNV).

Hebrew Names Version
This is a remake of the World English Bible Messianic Edition.

Conservative Bible Project
This Bible is rewritten to avoid passages that seem to condone sin, like the story of the adulteress in John 7:53-8:11.

David Robert Palmer Translation
The website was shut down at the time of this writing.

Restored Name King James Version
This is another sacred name version where the words for LORD and Jesus are replaced with a Hebrew word.

The Manga Bible
This is a children's story book of the Bible illustrated with Manga comics.

International Standard Version
This is a Messianic version Bible produced by the International Standard Version Foundation.

Ancient Word of God

English Jubilee 2000 Bible
This Bible was translated from Spanish into English by Russell Martin Stendal.

Young's Literal Revised Translation
This is a modern revision of the Young's Literal Translation of 1862.

Far Above All Bible
Graham G. Thomason translated this Bible.

Awful New Testament
This New Testament was written by Emery Szasz.

Modern American Standard Version
Dr. Maurice Robinson started this translation but abandoned it in favor of doing one from the Majority Text.

Transparent English Bible
James Tabor began his translation of the Bible by replacing "God" with "Elohim" in Genesis.

The Free Bible 2010
The website was shut down at the time of this writing.

The Disciples Bible 2011
The website was shut down at the time of this writing.

Victorious Gospel of Jesus Christ, New Covenant Translation
The website was shut down at the time of this writing.

Key Passages

Isaiah 7; Daniel 9; and Micah 5

The ancient church believed that Satan would try to tamper with the Scriptures in the last days. There are three key Old Testament passages we need to look at to determine if the translators truly understood the truths of Scripture and their importance in the last days. The key passages are Isaiah 7:14; Daniel 9:25-26; and Micah 5:2.

Isaiah 7:14

> Therefore the Lord Himself shall give you a sign;
> Behold, a <u>virgin</u> shall conceive, and bear a son,
> and shall call His name Immanuel. *Isaiah 7:14*

The gospel of Luke states this prophecy was fulfilled by Jesus, the Messiah, being born of Mary while she was still a virgin. Some have said the Hebrew word translated virgin in this verse is *alma* which means young woman. They say that if this passage meant virgin it would have used the Hebrew word *bethulah*. The opposite is true. In Joel 1:8, the word bethulah is used of a bride whose husband has died. In Jeremiah 51:22 and Psalm 148:12 bethulah is used to mean "young girl." In Psalm 78:63 bethulah is used to mean virgin. So bethulah can mean virgin, young girl, or bride. Alma is the only Hebrew word that anciently meant virgin. It is never used in any other way in the Hebrew Old Testament.

In the ancient Hebrew culture, all young women were either virgins or were stoned to death. A pregnant *young woman* is not a sign; but a pregnant *virgin* would be. The Peshitta (an Aramaic translation dated before AD 200) has the word bethulah instead of alma in Isaiah 7:14. The Greek Septuagint (the Greek Old Testament dated about 175 BC) used the Greek word *parthenos* in Isaiah 7:14, which can only mean virgin.

Irenaeus, *Against Heresies 3.21*, stated that the Septuagint used a Greek word that can only mean virgin for the Isaiah passage. This showed that the ancient Jews understood the word to mean virgin. With all this evidence, no Bible translation should have any word other than virgin.

Daniel 9:25-26

> Know therefore and understand, *that* from the going forth of the commandment to restore and to build Jerusalem unto the Messiah the Prince *shall be* seven weeks, and threescore and two weeks: the street shall be built again, and the wall, even in troublous times. *Daniel 9:25*

In this passage, Daniel predicted the coming of the Messiah. The ancient Seder Olam, a Jewish history book from AD 176, stated that Elijah the prophet would return and pave the way for King Messiah to save the Jews and Gentiles and set up a messianic rule on earth. Many ancient Jewish commentaries, ranging from Rashi to Maimonides, stated this passage referred to "the" Messiah.

Maimonides said:

> "Daniel has elucidated to us the knowledge of the
> end times. However, since they are secret, the
> wise [rabbis] have barred the calculation of the
> days of Messiah's coming so that the untutored
> populace will not be led astray when they see that
> the End Times have already come but there is no
> sign of the Messiah."
>
> *Maimonides: Igeret Teiman, Chapter 3*

In other words the Messiah was supposed to come about
AD 32 and the "wise" rabbis barred the reading of Daniel
9 because normal intelligent Jews would have accepted
Jesus as the Messiah and not suggested God was mistaken
when He sent the angel to tell Daniel the date the Messiah
would come. Jesus said in Matthew many deceivers will
come saying that they are christs. First John 2:22-23 and
5:1 teach Jesus is the *only* Christ.

No decent Bible translation should translate this passage
as "chosen leader," "elected official" or anything other
than Messiah or Christ; and preferably, *the* Messiah or *the*
Christ.

Micah 5:2

> But thou, Bethlehem Ephratah, *though* thou be
> little among the thousands of Judah, *yet* out of
> thee shall He come forth unto Me *that is* to be

ruler in Israel; whose goings forth *have been* <u>from of old, from everlasting</u>. *Micah 5:2*

This is a prophecy of Jesus being born in Bethlehem and that Jesus was "from eternity." First John quotes this as "from the beginning." This is a direct reference to the fact that Jesus is God and that He existed before any created thing. Since John uses this numerous times (1 John 1:1; 1:12; 1:14), it should be held as a key point of faith and translated as such. Phrases like "from eternity," "from the beginning," and "from everlasting" are acceptable. Phrases like "from long ago," or "from ancient times" are not acceptable because they don't show Jesus as God.

The LXX has "His goings forth were from the beginning, from days of eternity." The Geneva Bible has "whose goings forth have been from the beginning and from everlasting."

58 Bibles That Fail the Test

	Isaiah 7:14	Daniel 9:25-27	Micah 5:2
Original	**virgin**	**the Messiah**	**from eternity**
Thm	virgin	the Messiah	of an age
Leeser	young woman	the anointed	Ancient days
RV	virgin	anointed one	from everlasting
ASV	virgin	anointed one	from everlasting
EBR	virgin	anointed one	age-past time
Fenton	virgin	Messiah	old times
JPS	young woman	one anointed	ancient days
MRB	virgin	anointed one	ancient days
MNT	young woman		
AAT	young woman		
BBE	virgin	Messiah	long ago

Ancient Word of God

NWT	maiden	Messiah	time indefinite
RSV	young woman	an anointed one	ancient days
Knox	maid	Christ	ages untold
HSM	young woman	an anointed one	ancient days
AMP	virgin	anointed One	eternity
Knoch	damsel	Messiah	days eonian
JB	maiden	anointed prince	
NEB	young woman	one anointed	days gone by
NAB	virgin	one anointed	ancient times
TLB	virgin (girl)	anointed one	ages past
GNB	young woman	chosen leader	ancient times
NIV	virgin	anointed one	ancient times
NJB	young woman	anointed prince	days of old
NJPS	young woman		
NLV	young woman	the chosen one	the beginning
NRSV	young woman	anointed one	ancient days
REB	young woman	one anointed	ancient times
ERV	young woman	the chosen	ancient times
EVD	young woman	chosen king	long ago
NCV	virgin	appointed leader	days long ago
TEV	young girl	chosen leader	ancient times
GW	virgin	anointed prince	days long ago
CEV	virgin	chosen leader	ancient times
NIrV	virgin	anointed king	days of long ago
NLT	virgin	anointed One	distant past
CJB	young woman	anointed prince	in ancient times
TS98	maiden	Messiah	from everlasting
EEB	young woman		
ESV	virgin	an anointed one	ancient days
MSG	virgin	anointed leader	distinguished
ABP	virgin	anointed one	days of eon
CGV	girl	an anointed one	from everlasting
TNIV	virgin	anointed one	ancient times
NET	young woman	an anointed one	distant past
ACV	virgin	anointed one	from everlasting
ARTB	adolescent-girl	Messiah	forever
NETS	virgin	anointed leader	days of yore
TB	maiden	Messiah	from everlasting
NHEB	virgin	anointed prince	from everlasting
UPDV	young woman	anointed leader	from everlasting
NABRE	young woman		

EB	young woman	anointed leader	long ago
WEB	virgin	anointed one	from everlasting
WEB-ME	virgin	anointed one	from everlasting
HNV	virgin	anointed one	from everlasting
DRP	virgin	anointed one	from everlasting
Jubilee2000	virgin	anointed Prince	days of the ages

In addition to the fifty-eight Bibles that fail to translate the basic prophecies correctly, we have thirty-seven that were produced by a cult or an individual who is a non-trinitarian (the ancient church's definition of a cult). Easy reading / children's Bibles and paraphrases are not meant for serious study, so we remove them. Finally, we eliminate any edition which uses a Westcott and Hort Greek New Testament or an Old Testament that is based on any language other than Hebrew.

37 Cultic/Aberrant Bibles

Mace	Mace New Testament	Unitarian	1729
	Wakefield's New Testament	Unitarian	1791
	New Testament in an Improved Version	N-T	1808
JST	Joseph Smith Translation	Mormon	1844
	Emphatic Diaglott	Christa	1865
Noyes	New Testament	Unitarian	1869
Fenton	Ferrar Fenton Bible	BI	1903
Greber	The New Testament	Spiritist	1937
NWT	New World Translation	JW	1950
TANT	The Authentic New Testament	N-T	1955
HNB	Holy Name Bible	N-T	1963
	The New Testament: A New Translation	N-T	1968
BNT	Barkly New Testament	N-T	1968
LivEng	The Bible in Living English	JW	1972
SSBE	Sacred Scriptures (Bethal)	N-T	1981
ONT	Original New Testament	N-T	1985
KIT	Kingdom Interlinear Translation	JW	1985
CCB	Christian Community Bible	Liberal	1986
MCT	McCord's New Testament	Ch-Christ	1988

Ancient Word of God

	Clear Word Bible	SDA	1994
AST	Anointed Standard Translation	WS	1995
TS98	The Scriptures	N-T	1998
RcV	Recovery Version	Witness Lee	1999
	Last Days New Testament	Post	1999
	2001 Translation	N-T	2001
HSV	Holy Scriptures Version	Ch-Christ	2001
TWOY	The Word of Yahweh	N-T	2003
HRV	Hebraic-Roots Version	N-T	2004
NSB	New Simplified Bible	N-T	2004
TSNT	The Source New Testament	Liberal	2004
	Renovaré Spiritual Formation Bible	Emergent	2005
	Life with God Study Bible	Emergent	2005
	Spirit of Prophecy Study Bible	SDA	2006
TNB	Tarish Nephite Bible	Mormon	2008
	The Voice	Emergent	2008
TB	The Besorah (plagiarized '98 version)	N-T	2008
	The Victorious Gospel of Jesus Christ New Covenant Translation	Uni	-

JW: Jehovah's Witnesses; SDA: Seventh Day Adventists; Ch-Christ: Church of Christ
WS: White Supremacist groups; BI: British Israelite groups; Post: Post-tribulationist
N-T: Non-Trinitarian groups; Christa: Christadelphian; Uni: Universalist

15 Easy Reading/ Children's Bibles

BBE	Bible in Basic English	1949
NSNT	Norlie's Simplified New Testament	1961
CKJV	Children's King James Bible	1962
BWE	Bible in Worldwide English (NT)	1969
SEB	Simple English Bible	1980
	A New Accurate Translation	1984
NLV	New Life Version	1986
ERV	Easy-to-Read Version	1989
NCV	New Century Version	1991
Gaus	Unvarnished New Testament	1991
NIrV	New International Reader's Version	1996
TCE	The Common Edition New Testament	1999
EEB	Easy English Bible	2001
ICB	International Children's Bible	2007
MGB	The Manga Bible	2008

12 Paraphrases

	Doddridge's New Testament	1756
	Cotton Patch	1968
TSB	The Story Bible	1971
TLB	The Living Bible	1971
GNB	Good News Bible	1976
ERV	Easy-to-Read Version	1989
TEV	Today's English Version	1992
	Clear Word	1994
GW	God's Word	1995
CEV	Contemporary English Version	1995
MSG	The Message	2002
	Fresh Parenthetical Translation	2002

9 Westcott and Hort Translations

EBR	Rotherham's Emphasized Bible	1902
TCNT	Twentieth Century New Testament	1902
WNT	Weymouth New Testament	1903
CTNT	Centenary New Testament	1924
Knoch	Concordant Literal Version	1966
KJ20	King James Twentieth Century Version	1971
SNB	Restoration of Original Sacred Name Bible	1976
	Lattimore's New Testament	1996
OEB	Open English Bible	2009

32 Septuagint, Vulgate, and Aramaic Bibles

	Wycliffe	Vulgate	1382
	Tyndale New Testament*	Vulgate	1526
	Coverdale	Vulgate	1535
	Matthew*	Vulgate	1537
	Great Bible	Vulgate	1537
	Taverner	Vulgate	1539
	Bishops Bible	Vulgate	1568
DR	Douai-Rheims	Vulgate	1582
DRC	Challoner's Revision of the D-R	Vulgate	1752
Thm	Thomson's Translation	LXX	1808
Ethridge	Ethridge's Peshitta	Aramaic	1849
	Brenton's Septuagint	LXX	1851
Murdock	Murdock's Peshitta	Aramaic	1852

WVSS	Westminster Version of Sacred Scriptures*	Vulgate	1913
Lamsa	Lamsa Bible	Aramaic	1933
SPC	Spencer New Testament	Vulgate	1941
CCD	Confraternity Bible*	Vulgate	1941
Knox	Knox's Translation of the Vulgate	Vulgate	1955
JB	Jerusalem Bible*	Vulgate	1966
NJB	New Jerusalem Bible*	Vulgate	1985
CCB	Christian Community Bible*	Vulgate	1986
	2001 Translation	LXX	2001
ABP	Apostolic Bible Polyglot	LXX	2003
AB	Apostles' Bible	LXX	2004
Younan	Younan's Peshitta Interlinear	Aramaic	2004
CAB	Complete Apostles' Bible	LXX	2005
NETS	New English Translation of the Septuagint	LXX	2007
OSB	Orthodox Study Bible	LXX	2007
WGCIB	Work of God's Children Illustrated Bible	Vulgate	2010
EOB	Eastern/Greek Orthodox Bible	LXX	2010
TFB	The Free Bible	LXX	2010
AAEB	An American English Bible	LXX	2011

*partly on Vulgate or LXX

This leaves the following 81 Bibles from our Master list.

Abbrev	Name	Date
	Geneva	1560
KJV	Authorized King James	1611
Whiston	Whiston's Primitive New Testament	1745
Wesley	Wesley's New Testament	1760
Quaker	Anthony Purver Bible	1764
Webster	Webster's Revision	1833
LONT	Living Oracles New Testament	1835
YLT	Young's Literal Translation	1862
Anderson	Anderson's 1865 New Testament	1865
Julia	Julia E. Smith Parker Translation	1876
DBY	Darby Bible	1890
Godbey	Godbey New Testament	1902
WAS	Worrell New Testament	1904
RNT	Riverside New Testament	1923
MRB	Modern Reader's Bible	1923
WmNT	Williams New Testament	1937
KLNT	Kleist-Lilly New Testament	1956
PME	Phillips New Testament in Modern English	1958

BV	The Berkeley Version	1958
WET	Wuest Expanded Translation	1961
TDB	The Dartmouth Bible	1961
NNT	Noli New Testament	1961
MLB	Modern Language Bible	1969
TBR	The Bible Reader	1969
KJII	King James II	1971
NASB	New American Standard Bible	1971
BECK	An American Translation	1976
IB	Interlinear Bible (Green)	1976
NKJV	New King James Version	1982
NJPS	New Jewish Publication Society of America	1985
LITV	Green's Literal Translation	1985
JNT	Jewish New Testament	1989
GNC	God's New Covenant (NT)	1989
KJ21	21st Century King James	1991
AIV	An Inclusive Version	1995
TMB	Third Millennium Bible	1998
MKJV	Modern King James Version	1999
AKJV	American King James Version	1999
ALT	Analytical-Literal Translation	1999
UKJV	Updated King James Version	2000
KJV2000	King James 2000 Version	2000
SSFOY	Sacred Scriptures, Family of Yah Edition	2000
RKJNT	Revised King James New Testament	2000
KJVER	King James Version Easy Reading	2001
UTV	Urim Thummim Version	2001
WV	Wycliffe Version (Noble)	2001
OJB	Orthodox Jewish Bible	2002
HNC	Holy New Covenant	2002
CKJV	Comfort-able King James Version	2003
EMTV	English Majority Text Version	2003
FNT	Faithful New Testament	2003
VW	A Voice In The Wilderness Holy Scriptures	2003
HCSB	Holman Christian Standard Bible	2004
TNIV	Today's New International Version	2005
NCPB	New Cambridge Paragraph Bible	2005
SN-KJ	Sacred Name King James Bible	2005
KJ3	KJ3—Literal Translation Bible	2005
WNT	William's New Testament	2005
UVNT	Understandable Version NT	2005
ChB	Christolog Bible	2005
AV7	AV7 (New Authorized Version)	2006
AVU	Authorized Version Update	2006
ICB	International Children's Bible	2007

Ancient Word of God

NIBEV	Natural Israelite Bible, English Version	2007
COM	The Comprehensive New Testament	2008
HOB	Holy Orthodox Bible	2008
ANT	Accurate New Testament	2008
CPDV	Catholic Public Domain Version	2009
LEB	Lexham English Bible	2010
NABRE	New American Bible Revised Edition	2011
MLV	Modern Literal Version	2011
DB	Disciple's Bible	2011
TrLB	Tree of Life Bible	2011
CBP	Conservative Bible Project	-
RNKJV	Restored Name King James Version	-
ISV	International Standard Version	-
YRT	Young's Revised Translation	-
FAA	Far Above All Version	-
Szasz	Awful New Testament (Emery Szasz)	-
MASV	Modern American Standard Version	-
TEB	Transparent English Bible	-

- Internet based or not yet published

Luke 1-2; 1 Timothy 3

There are three New Testament passages we should use to check our remaining Bibles against: Luke 1:27; Luke 2:33; and 1 Timothy 3:16.

Luke 1:27

> To a <u>virgin</u> espoused to a man whose name was Joseph, of the house of David; and the virgin's name *was* Mary. *Luke 1:27*

We have already looked at why Isaiah 7:14 should be translated virgin. Chapter one of Luke clearly states that Mary was a virgin and that her being a virgin was a fulfillment of the prophecy of Isaiah. Therefore, this verse, too, must be translated virgin. Any Bible translating it as "young woman" or "wife" is in error.

Luke 2:33

> And <u>Joseph</u> and his mother marvelled at those things which were spoken of him. *Luke 2:33*

With the Gospels clearly teaching the virgin birth of Jesus, we know that Mary is His real biological mother and Joseph is not His real biological father. Since Mary's virginity is a main point of doctrine and one of the most important prophecies, the New Testament would never state that Joseph was Jesus' father. Luke 2:33 should always be translated as found in the received text: "Joseph and his mother," not "His mother and father." Corrupt Bibles state "the child's mother and father" or "the child's parents" in this verse. Joseph is never referred to as Jesus' father *anywhere* in Scripture. Some have used what Mary said to make this seem all right.

> And when they saw him, they were amazed: and his mother said unto him, Son, why hast thou thus dealt with us? behold, thy father and I have sought thee sorrowing. And he said unto them, How is it that ye sought me? wist ye not that I must be about my Father's business? *Luke 2:48-49*

This verse simply records what Mary said when in a panic thinking she had lost her son. Notice Jesus *corrects* her, stating He was about his *real* Father's business. All accurate Bibles will have "Joseph," not "father," in Luke 2:33.

1 Timothy 3:16

> And without controversy great is the mystery of godliness: <u>God</u> was manifest in the flesh, justified in the Spirit, seen of angels, preached unto the Gentiles, believed on in the world, received up into glory. *1 Timothy 3:16*

In ancient times it was very costly to produce copies of Scripture, so the scribes invented abbreviations for words like God, Lord, Jesus, Holy Spirit, etc. They abbreviated the word for God, *theos*, by just using the "th" and the "s." The abbreviations have a line above the word so the reader will not be confused. It looks like this $\overline{\Theta\Sigma}$. The normal word for "who" is ΟΣ. These look nearly identical. So, is there any evidence of a smudged out line in or above the abbreviation for theos?

Yes! There are over 300 manuscripts that clearly show the line in the theta, Θ. There are reported to be only four Greek manuscripts that show ΟΣ without the line in the Theta. These are the Sinaiticus, Alexandrinus, Ephraemi Rescriptus, and Miniscule 33. These are so smudged and overwritten it would be hard to tell what they have. For example, here is 1 Timothy 3:16 from the Codex Ephraemi.

Codex Ephraemi - 1 Timothy 3:16

God manifested in the flesh would be perfect Greek grammar for this sentence. If we change the word God, $\overline{\Theta\Sigma}$, to who, ΟΣ, ΟΣ would be a masculine relative pronoun modifying the neuter noun "mystery," which would create a clause with a predicate and no subject. This would be extremely poor Greek grammar. Nouns and pronouns must have the same ending: masculine, feminine, or neuter.

First Timothy 3:16 seems to be a different subject, not fitting with 1 Timothy 3:1-5, which teaches about the qualifications of pastors and deacons. But it does fit perfectly with First Timothy 4:1-6 which states "if" you teach others these things, you will be a good minister. What things? That forced celibacy and vegetarianism are doctrines of demons and that God was manifested in the flesh. Theologically, this verse only makes sense if it says God, not "who."

Several ancient church fathers either quote or allude to this passage. Ignatius (AD 100), in his *Epistle to the Ephesians* quotes "God manifested in the flesh" twice. Dionysius (AD 265) quotes the full verse in *Concilia i. 858a.* Hippolytus (AD 210) in his *Against Noetus,* paraphrases this passage at least three times. Chrysostom (AD 350) quotes the passage in full several times throughout his discourses and homilies. Gregory of Nyssa (AD 370) quotes this passage in Greek at least twenty-two times!

For a complete study on 1 John 5:7-8, see the next chapter. It is included in the chart below to show that the same Bibles classified corrupt for other reasons usually do not include 1 John 5:7-8.

48 Bibles That Fail the Test

	Luke 1:27	Luke 2:33	1 Tim. 3:16	1 John 5:7
Original	**virgin**	**Joseph**	**God**	**included**
Vulgate	virgin	father	which	-omitted-
Wycliffe	virgin	father	that they	included
Tyndale	virgin	father	God	included
Coverdale	virgin	father	God	included
Whiston	virgin	father	who	-omitted-

LONT	virgin	parents	he who	-omitted-
Anderson	virgin	Joseph	God	-omitted-
Etheridge	virgin	Joseph	which	included
Murdock	virgin	Joseph	which	included
DBY	virgin	father	God	-omitted-
Godbey	virgin	father	who	-omitted-
WAS	virgin	father	God/who	-omitted-
RNT	virgin	parents	who	-omitted-
MRB	virgin	father	-	-
Lamsa	virgin	Joseph	it	-omitted-
WmNT	virgin	father	he	-omitted-
KLNT				-omitted-
PME	young woman	father	the one	-omitted-
BV	virgin	father	he	-omitted-
WET	virgin	father	who	-omitted-
MLB	virgin	father	he	-omitted-
KJ20	maiden	father	he	-omitted-
NASB	virgin	father	he	-omitted-
TLB	virgin	Joseph	who	-garbled-
BECK				-omitted-
NIV	virgin	father	he	-omitted-
NJPS	virgin	father		
CCB	virgin	father	he	-omitted-
MCT	virgin	father	he	-omitted-
JNT	virgin	father		-omitted-
GNC	young woman	father	he	-omitted-
NLT	virgin	parents	Christ	-omitted-
TCE	virgin	father	he	-omitted-
SSFOY	virgin	father	he	-omitted-
OJB	virgin	father	who	-omitted-
HNC	virgin girl	father	Christ	-omitted-
FNT	virgin	father	God	-omitted-
HCSB	virgin	father	he	-omitted-
UVNT	virgin	stepfather	God or who	-omitted-
CPDV	virgin	father	which	included
UPDV	wife	father	he	-omitted-
LEB	virgin	father	who	-omitted-
LONT	virgin	Joseph	he	-omitted-
RKJNT	virgin	father	he	-omitted-
RNKJV	virgin	Joseph	who	-omitted-
ISV	virgin	father	he	-omitted-

| NABRE | virgin | father | who | -omitted- |
| TrLB | virgin | father | he | -omitted- |

25 Bibles Not Used for Other Reasons

Quaker Julia KLNT BECK	Hard-to-find, rare Bibles: therefore these can't make a good study Bible. KLNT is an older Catholic Bible. BECK contains the adulteress story (John 7-8) but foot notes that it was not in the original gospel of John.
AKJV UKJV KJVCNT	These KJV updates were created by a single individual who changed the endings or a few of the archaic words. E.g. "saith" to "says"
Julia Szasz	Woody, Mechanical, hard to understand.
AIV	This feminist Bible changes God the Father to Father-Mother. Jesus is not the Son of God, but the Child of the divine.
NCPB	Based on the 1611 KJV and Bishop's Bible with Apocrypha. This edition has eliminated italicized words.
COM	Adds notes from pagan sources to expound the text.
TMB	A modernized KJV with Apocrypha. (Thou, Ye)
AVU	Based on the TR and MT combined.
AV7	Gender inclusive (ex. 1 Tim. 2:4).
SN-JV	Odd word replacement, God with ELOHIYM or EL and Jesus Christ with YAHSHUA MASHIYACH.
KJV2000	Red letter for trinity Old and New Testaments; paraphrases on occasion (You).
Wesley	This NT was so similar to the KJV that now only *Wesley's notes on the New Testament* is produced.
TDB	One half of this KJV content has been edited away.
WNT	Omitted the adulteress story (John 7-8).
UTV	Adds the book of Enoch to the canon.
ChB	Another sacred name KJV makeover.
NIBEV	Another sacred name KJV makeover.
CBP	Removed passages like the adulteress (John 8).
MTyndale	Modern Tyndale is not a complete New Testament.

This leaves the following 21 Bibles from our list.

Abbrev	Name	Date
	Geneva	1560
KJV	Authorized King James	1611
Webster	Webster's Revision	1833
YLT	Young's Literal Translation	1862
NNT	Noli New Testament	1961
KJII	King James II	1971
IB	Interlinear Bible (Green)	1976
NKJV	New King James Version	1982
LITV	Green's Literal Translation	1985
KJ21	21st Century King James	1991
MKJV	Modern King James Version	1999
ALT	Analytical-Literal Translation	1999
KJVER	King James Version Easy Reading	2001
EMTV	English Majority Text Version	2003
VW	A Voice In The Wilderness Holy Scriptures	2003
KJ3	KJ3—Literal Translation Bible	2005
HOB	Holy Orthodox Bible	2008
MLV	Modern Literal Version	2011
DB	Disciple's Bible	2011
YRT	Young's Revised Translation	-
FAA	Far Above All Version	-

- Internet based or not yet published

1 John 5:7-8

For there are three that bear record in heaven, the Father, the Word, and the Holy Ghost: and these three are one. And there are three that bear witness in earth, the Spirit, and the water, and the blood: and these three agree in one. *1 John 5:7-8*

Most modern Bibles have the first grayed out part for their verse 7 and the second grayed out part for their verse 8, leaving out the middle part. The middle disputed part is called the Johannine Comma.

Manuscript Evidence

Only 300 of the 5,300 plus manuscripts have 1 John. Of these 300, only ten Greek manuscripts ranging from the fourteenth century to the eighteenth century, contain the Johannine Comma; Manuscripts 61, 629, 918, 2318, 2473, 88, 177, 221, 429, 636. Nine Latin manuscripts, ranging from the 10th to 16th centuries include the Comma. These facts are used by some scholars to teach that the Comma was never in the original text of 1 John. But let's reverse these facts. The Critical Text advocates always say we should disregard Greek manuscripts past the tenth century because they are merely copies of earlier ones. With that in mind, how many ancient Greek manuscripts do *not* contain the Johannine Comma? Four! Yes, there are only four pre-tenth century manuscripts that do not contain the missing middle section of 1 John 5 to even be considered.

Theology

First John 5:9-10 refer to the event recorded in Matthew 17:5 where God the Father spoke out of heaven and testified that Jesus was His Son.

If we leave the Comma in, we have the witness of the Trinity and the witness of man in verses 7-8. Verse 9 contrasts the witness of men, described in verses 6 and 8 with the witness of God in verse 7 and 10-11. If we leave out the Comma, we have verses 10-11 referring back to a non-existent clause.

It is amazing that the Alexandrian text "experts" reject "God" in 1 Timothy 3:16, in spite of the fact that all but the Sinaiticus and possibly three other smudged manuscripts show "he." These same experts reject the Johannine Comma despite the fact that nineteen manuscripts contain it and only four do not.

Church Father Quotes

Several ancient church fathers quote or allude to this passage. Cyprian says:

> The Lord says, 'I and the Father are one;' [John 10:30] and again it is written of the Father, and of the Son, and of the Holy Spirit, 'and these three are one' [1 John 5:7-8].
> Cyprian, *Unity of the Church 6*, AD 250

Jerome commented in his Latin Vulgate that the Greek church created a controversy when they decided to leave out the Johannine Comma. His Greek copies, now non-existent, contained the Johannine Comma and he refused to alter the Scriptures!

> The general epistles are not the same in the Greek Church as they are for the Latin Church... These general epistles have been correctly understood and faithfully translated into Latin [from the Greek] in their entirety, without ambiguous or missing information; especially the verse about the unity of the Trinity found in 1 John. Unfaithful translators have created much controversy by omitting the phrase "Father, Word, and Spirit," while leaving the phrase "water, blood and spirit," which only serves to strengthen our faith and show the Father, Son, and Holy Spirit are of the same substance. I do not fear those who call me a corrupter of Scriptures; I *refuse* to deny the truth of Scripture to those who seek it.
>
> Jerome, *Prologue to the Canonical Epistles*, Codex Fuldensis, AD 541-546

Why would the Greek church decide to remove the Johannine Comma? There are plenty of verses that teach the doctrine of the Trinity; but a heresy arose in the east called Sabellianism or Praxianism, named after the heretics Sabellius and Praxeas. Praxeas taught Jesus was an incarnation of the Father, much like Oneness[q] groups do today. Praxeas would have, no doubt, used 1 John 5:7 to assert his heresy. Tertullian stated that 1 John 5:7 is saying these three are one in substance, and this is what Jesus meant when He said that He and the Father are One in John 10:30. Jesus did not mean He was the Father.

"'These Three are one' in essence, not one Person, as it is said, 'I and My Father are One,' in respect of unity of substance, not singularity of number." Tertullian *Against Praxeas 25*, AD 200

The writings of Tertullian predate the oldest Biblical Greek manuscripts (Sinaticus and Vaticanus) by well over 150 years!

We have 86,000 quotes of Scripture from the ancient church fathers (AD 32-325). Here are just a few of the ones who either quoted, or alluded to, the Johannine Comma.

1. 215, Tertullian, *Against Praxeas 25*
2. 250, Cyprian, *Unity of the Church 6*
3. 250, Cyprian, *Epistle to Jubaianus*
4. 635, Athanasius, *Books 1 & 10*, cited three times
5. 380, Priscillian, *Liber Apologeticus*
6. 385, Gregory of Nazianzus, *Theological Orientations (Holy Spirit)*
7. 390, Jerome, *Prologue to the General Epistles*

---

[q] Oneness groups reject the doctrine of the Trinity by teaching the Jesus is God the Father.

8. 450, Author Unknown, *De divinis Scripturis suie Spaculum*
9. 500, Jerome, *Codex Freisingensis*
10. 527, Flugentius, *De Trinitate*

In AD 638 Muslims destroyed the Library of Caesarea, which was said to contain 30,000 volumes and was used by Origen, Eusebius, and Jerome. No one knows how many Greek New Testament Manuscripts were in that library.

There are still thousands of old Latin manuscripts that have never been examined. Codex Teplensis is one Old Latin manuscript that contains the Comma.

For an exhaustive study on 1 John 5:7-8, see *The Debate Over 1 John 5:7-8*, by Michael Maynard.

The *Greek Orthodox New Testament* (abbreviated GONT), the official Greek Text used by the Greek Orthodox Church, was published in 1904. It is closer to the Received Text than the Majority Text, but still has major differences. It does contain 1 John 5:7-8 exactly as it appears in the Received Text. However, the English translations that are supposedly based upon it have chosen not to include 1 John 5:7-8 for some unknown reason.

7 Byzantine-Based Bibles

	Luke 1:27	Luke 2:33	1 Timothy 3:16	1 John 5:7
GO-1904	**Virgin**	**Joseph**	**God**	**-included-**
Noli	virgin	Joseph	God	-included-
MLV	virgin	Joseph	God	-omitted-
HOB	virgin	Joseph	God	-omitted-
MT-2005	virgin	Joseph	God	-omitted-
ALT	virgin	Joseph	God	-omitted-
EMTV	virgin	Joseph	God	-omitted-
FAA	virgin	Joseph	God	-omitted-
DB	virgin	Joseph	God	-omitted-

Constantinople Official Greek Text, GONT, is based on 20 key manuscripts, while the MT is based on 400 somewhat fragmented older manuscripts.

Conclusion

Removing the remaining MT- based Bibles which do not have 1 John 5:7-8, leaves us with only twelve good Bible translations.

12 TR Based Bibles

	Luke 1:27	Luke 2:33	1 Timothy 3:16	1 John 5:7
Original	**virgin**	**Joseph**	**God**	**-included-**
Geneva	virgin	Ioseph	God	-included-
KJV	virgin	Joseph	God	-included-
Webster	virgin	Joseph	God	-included-
YLT	virgin	Joseph	God	-included-
KJII/MKJV*	virgin	Joseph	God	-included-
IB	virgin	Joseph	God	-included-
NKJV	virgin	Joseph	God	-included-
LITV/KJ3*	virgin	Joseph	God	italicized
KJ21	virgin	Joseph	God	-included-
KJVER	virgin	Joseph	God	-included-
VW	virgin	Joseph	God	-included-
YLR	virgin	Joseph	God	-included-

* The King James II was republished as the Modern King James Version and the LITV was republished as the KJ3.

The Twelve

The twelve good Bibles are the Geneva Bible, King James Version, Webster Bible, Young's Literal Translation, Modern King James, Green's Interlinear Bible, New King James Version, KJ3, 21st Century King James Version, King James Version Easy Reading, Voice in the Wilderness Scriptures, and the Young's Literal Revised Edition.

Study Bibles

Having exhausted the study on Bible versions, we need to take a moment to consider study Bibles. A study Bible may come in various versions, like KJV, NASB, and NIV. So we need to consider the *notes* in the study Bible. We may have a good version but a bad set of notes or a corrupt version but a wonderful set of notes. Both may be inadequate. We need to find a study Bible with an excellent translation and excellent study notes.

Our primary study Bible should be a Bible based on the Received Text. Only two of the twelve Bibles based on the Received Text are used today in Study Bibles. Our only choice is the KJV or NKJV, except in the case of the Interlinear Bible of J. P. Green, which uses the LITV.

We have listed here for you a master list of seventy-three Study Bibles.

Study Bibles

	Bible		Type
1	Apologetics Study Bible	HCSB	A
2	Archaeological Study Bible	NIV, KJV	
3	Blackaby Study Bible	NKJV	
4	Cambridge Annotated Study Bible	NRSV	L
5	Case for Christ Study Bible	NIV	
6	Catholic Study Bible	NAB	L, Ca
7	Catholic Bible: Personal Study Ed.	NAB	L, Ca

8	Chronological Study Bible	NKJV	
9	Companion Bible	KJV,NKJV	D
10	Dake*	KJV	P
11	Dickson New Analytical Study Bible	KJV	O
12	Disciple's Study Bible	NIV	Ev
13	ESV Study Bible	ESV	C
14	Essential Study Bible	CEV	
15	Evidence Bible	KJV	
16	Everyday Life Bible	AMP	
17	Expositor's Study Bible	KJV	P
18	Fire Bible		P
19	Full Life Study Bible	KJV,NIV	P
20	Harper Study Bible	NASB,NRSV	Ev
21	Harper-Collins Study Bible	NRSV	L
22	Hebrew-Greek Key Word Study Bible	KJV,NASB	Ev
23	Holman Christian Standard Bible	HCSB	
24	Ignatius Catholic Study Bible	RSV	Ca
25	Inductive Study Bible	NASB	
26	Inspirational Study Bible	NKJV	
27	KJV Matthew Henry Study Bible	KJV	C, Dv
28	KJV Study Bible	KJV	
29	Life Application Bible	KJV,LB,NIV, NKJV,NASB	Ev
30	Life Essentials Study Bile	HCSB	
31	Life in the Spirit Study Bible	KJV,NIV	P,A
32	Life Principles Study Bible	NKJV,NASB	C,Dv
33	Life Recovery Bible (12 Step)	NLT	N
34	Life with God Study Bible	NRSV	E
35	Lucado Life Lessons Study Bible	NKJV	Dv
36	Lutheran Study Bible	ESV	
37	Matthew Henry Study Bible	KJV	
38	Maxwell Leadership Bible	NKJV	L, C
39	McArthur Study Bible	NASB,ESV	C
40	Mission of God Study Bible		C
41	NASB Study Bible	NASB	C
42	New Believer's Bible	NLT	
43	New Inductive Study Bible	NASB	
44	NIV Study Bible	NIV	C,Ev
45	New Interpreter's Study Bible	NRSV	L
46	New Geneva Study Bible	NKJV	C
47	New Jerusalem Bible	NJB	L,Ca

48	NKJV Study Bible	NKJV	
49	NLT Study Bible	NLT	
50	New Open Bible	KJV,NASB,NKJV	O
51	New Oxford Annotated Bible	NRSV	L
52	New Scofield Study Bible	KJV,NIV,NASB,NKJV	C
53	New Spirit-Filled Life Bible	NKJV	P
54	New Student Bible	NIV,NRSV	Ev
55	Orthodox Study Bible	NKJV	O
56	Oxford Study Bible	REB	L
57	Prophecy Study Bible	KJV, NKJV	
58	Quest Study Bible	NIV	Ev
59	Rainbow Study Bible	KJV,LB,NIV	
60	Reformation Study Bible	ESV	C
61	Renovaré *	NRSV	E
62	Revival Study Bible*	NKJV	W-F
63	Ryrie Study Bible	KJV,NIV,NASB	D
64	Scofield Study Bible	KJV	C,D
65	Serendipity Study Bible	NIV	
66	Spirit-Filled Life Bible	KJV,NKJV	P
67	Thompson Chain Reference	KJV,NIV,NASB,NKJV	O
68	Transformation Study Bible	NLT	
69	Wesley Bible	NKJV	A
70	Word in Life Study Bible	NKJV,NRSV	Ev
71	Word For Today Bible	NKJV	
72	The Word Study Bible*	KJV	P,W-F

L: Liberal; C: Calvinist; P: Pentecostal; W-F: Word Faith; Ca: Catholic; A: Arminian;
E: Emergent; O: Orthodox; D: Dispensational; Ev: Evangelical; O: Object Orientated;
S: Subject Orientated; N: Needs Orientated; Dv: Devotional

*Not recommended for study

If we take only the Received Text based Bibles (KJV, NKJV, LITV) and remove study Bibles that are overtly Calvinistic, Roman Catholic, Liberal, or non-trinitarian in doctrine and those that are so much of a "devotional" nature that they take away the focus from God to people, we have the following:

Ancient Word of God

Archaeological Study Bible
This has good general information on archeological finds that support various places, people, and customs mentioned in the Bible.

Blackaby Study Bible
Dr. Henry Blackaby produced this study Bible. He is also the co-author of *Experiencing God.*

Chronological Study Bible
This Bible takes the text of Scripture and rearranges it into chronological order. This may help in understanding the historical order in which events took place, but it would not be recommended for a primary study Bible.

Companion Bible
This is a KJV with notes organized in a similar fashion to the Thompson Chain Reference Bible. It was developed by E. W. Bullinger in late 1800's.

Dake
This Bible was put together by an Assemblies of God minister who believed the Father has a body and that Jesus did not become the Christ until His baptism.

Dickson Study Bible
This study Bible is no longer in print.

Evidence Bible
This Bible comes with notes on subjects pertinent to witnessing to unbelievers (Way of the Master), cults, and answering hard life questions new believers ask.

Expositor's Study Bible
This Bible was put out by Jimmy Swaggart Ministries. It seems overly full of notes.

Full Life Study Bible
This Bible was created by Pentecostal missionary Donald C. Stamps. It is now out of print but has been replaced by the *Life in the Spirit Study Bible*.

Hebrew-Greek Key Word Study Bible
Greek-speaking Spiros Zodhiates edited this Bible, underlining key words in each verse that are referenced to Strong's reference numbers. It also indicates the Greek tenses of key New Testament words.

Inspirational Study Bible
This is a devotional Study Bible by Max Lucado who has a Churches of Christ background. This was basically replaced by the *Lucado Life Lessons Study Bible*.

KJV Study Bible
This is the standard Study Bible for the KJV, by Thomas Nelson, originally published by Liberty University (Jerry Falwell).

Ancient Word of God

Life Application Study Bible
This is the current standard for devotional Bibles.

Life in the Spirit Study Bible
This is the update to the out-of-print *Full Life Study Bible*.

Life Principles Study Bible
This devotional Study Bible was created by Dr. Charles Stanley.

Lucado Life Lessons Study Bible
This is a devotional Study Bible by Max Lucado which replaced the Inspirational Study Bible.

Maxwell Leadership Bible
This Bible was created by John C. Maxwell, a student of Robert Schuller.

NKJV Study Bible
This is the standard Study Bible for the NKJV, by Thomas Nelson.

New Open Bible
This study Bible has fewer notes than the KJV or NKJV study Bibles, but has a very nice cyclopedia index that is its main feature. It also contains book outlines and charts.

New Spirit-Filled Life Bible
This Pentecostal study Bible was produced by Jack Hayford of the Foursquare Church.

Orthodox Study Bible
This study Bible's New Testament is NKJV but its Old Testament is a translation of the Septuagint.

Prophecy Study Bible
This sounds wonderful, but it seems to have relatively few prophecy notes in it. One might be better off buying another KJV or NKJV along with a good book on Bible prophecy like *Ancient Prophecies Revealed.*

Rainbow Study Bible
This Bible has a color-coded system for each verse indicating whether the verse is talking about prophecy, salvation, God's nature, etc.

Revival Study Bible
This Bible contains questionable articles from people like Benny Hinn, Smith Wigglesworth, etc.

Ryrie Study Bible
This Bible's notes came from Dr. Charles Ryrie an ardent premillennialist, pre-tribulationist, dispensationalist, non-Calvinist, and an adherent to the doctrine of eternal security.

Spirit-Filled Life Bible
Jack Hayford's Pentecostal study Bible is not out print, but it has been replaced by the *New Spirit-Filled Life Bible.*

Ancient Word of God

Thompson Chain-Reference
Frank Charles Thompson, a Methodist, created a system that takes you from one verse to another to learn major Bible Doctrines.

Wesley Study Bible
This NKJV study Bible seems to be out of print. The NRSV Wesley Study Bible by the same name is still in print.

Word in Life Study Bible
Out of print

Word For Today Bible
This study Bible is produced by Chuck Smith of Calvary Chapel.

The Word Study Bible
This is a Word-Faith Study Bible with articles by questionable teachers.

Recommended Study Bibles

1	Archaeological Study Bible	KJV	
2	Blackaby Study Bible		NKJV
3	Companion Bible	KJV	NKJV
4	Evidence Bible	KJV	
5	Hebrew-Greek Key Word Study Bible	KJV	
6	KJV Study Bible	KJV	
7	Life Application Study Bible	KJV	NKJV
8	Life in the Spirit Study Bible	KJV	
9	NKJV Study Bible		NKJV
10	New Open Bible	KJV	NKJV
11	New Student Bible	KJV	
12	New Spirit-Filled Life Bible		NKJV
13	Ryrie Study Bible	KJV	
14	Thompson Chain-Reference	KJV	NKJV
15	Word For Today Bible		NKJV

Ancient Word of God

Commentaries and Dictionaries

Here is a master list of commentaries and dictionaries. Again, we removed any that were created by people or groups that were cultic, Calvinistic, Roman Catholic, and those who do not believe in inerrancy.

Commentaries

John Gill	Calvinistic Baptist, Pro 1 John 5:7
Keil & Delitzsch	Creationist, fundamentalist
Jamieson, Fausset and Brown	Anglican
Darby	Dispensational, anti-Catholic
Matthew Henry	Presbyterian
Summarized Bible	Keith L. Brooks - Moody
Nave's Topical Bible	Nave - Methodist
Torrey's Topical Textbook	R. A. Torrey - Congregationalist

Not Recommended	
Albert Barnes	Presbyterian, evolutionist
People's New Testament	BW Johnson Campbellite, Preterist [t]
Clarke[r]	British Methodist
Scofield Notes[s]	Cyrus Scofield - Presbyterian
Nazarene Commentary 2000	Non-trintarian
Expositor's Bible Commentary	Denies 1 John 5:7-8 is Scripture

---

[r] Clarke was Anti-Roman Catholic, Anti-Semitic, preterist, denied the eternal sonship of Jesus, saying Jesus did not exist prior to His incarnation.

[s] Cyrus Scofield - Calvinistic, premillennial, dispensational, denied 1 John 5:7-8 was Scripture

[t] Non-premillennialist

Dictionaries

Webster's 1828 Dictionary	Noah Webster - Congregationalist
Robinson Word Pictures	A. T. Robertson - Southern Baptist
Easton's Dictionary	M.G. Easton - Scottish Presbyterian
Thayer's Greek Definitions	Thayer taught theological inerrancy*
Strong's Greek and Hebrew	James Strong - Methodist

*Theological Inerrancy teaches that the Bible is 100% accurate in theology but not in history or science.

Appendices

A.
Majority Text vs. Received Text

The following list shows, some examples where the MT omits or changes a minor point of the text that probably *does not* change any doctrine.

1. Matt. 4:18 - (TR) Jesus (MT) He
2. Matt. 5:27 - (TR) of them of old time (MT) *omitted*
3. Matt. 5:47 - (TR) brethren (MT) friends
4. Matt. 8:5 - (TR) Jesus (MT) He
5. Matt. 8:25 - (TR) His disciples (MT) disciples
6. Matt. 14:22 - (TR) His disciples (MT) disciples
7. Mark 8:14 - (TR) the disciples (MT) they
8. Mark 9:7 - (TR) saying (MT) *omitted*
9. Luke 2:21 - (TR) the child (MT) Him
10. Luke 3:19 - (TR) Philip's (MT) his brother
11. Luke 7:31 - (TR) and the Lord said (MT) *omitted*
12. Luke 9:1 - (TR) disciples (MT) *omitted*
13. Luke 20:19 - (TR) feared the people (MT) were afraid [u]
14. John 1:29 - (TR) John seeth (MT) he saw
15. John 1:43 - (TR) Jesus (MT) He
16. Acts 9:28 - (TR) and going out (MT) *omitted*
17. Acts 9:38 - (TR) Joppa (MT) there
18. Acts 9:38 - (TR) two men (MT) *omitted*
19. Acts 10:21 - (TR) were sent unto him from Cornelius (MT) *omitted*
20. Acts 13:17 - (TR) of Israel (MT) our fathers
21. Acts 13:24 - (TR) to all the people of Israel (MT) to Israel

---

[u] Both TR and MT have "Feared the people" in Matt. 21:46

22. Acts 24:6 - (TR) judged according to our law (MT) arrested
23. Romans 16:25-27 - the MT places these verses after Romans 14:23 as Romans 14:24-26, but the words are identical
24. 1 Corinthians 15:39 - (TR) flesh of men (MT) of men
25. Hebrews 12:20 - (TR) or thrust through with a dart (MT) *omitted* [v]
26. Rev. 4:3 - (TR) And He that sat was (MT) *omitted*
27. Rev. 5:4 - (TR) and to read the book (MT) *omitted*
28. Rev. 5:7 - (TR) the book (MT) *omitted*
29. Rev. 5:14 - (TR) four and twenty elders (MT) elders
30. Rev. 6:3 - (TR) and see (MT) *omitted*
31. Rev. 6:5 - (TR) and see (MT) *omitted*
32. Rev. 6:7 - (TR) and see (MT) *omitted*
33. Rev. 7:4 - (TR) 144,000 (MT) 144,000 *spelled out*
34. Rev. 8:7 - (TR) first angel (MT) first
35. Rev. 8:8 - (TR) burning (MT) *omitted*
36. Rev. 9:4 - (TR) only (MT) *omitted*
37. Rev. 11:1 - (TR) and the angel stood, saying (MT) *omitted*
38. Rev. 13:18 - (TR) 666 (MT) 666 spelled out
39. Rev. 14:5 - (TR) before the throne of God (MT) *omitted*
40. Rev. 16:4 - (TR) third angel (MT) third
41. Rev. 16:10 - (TR) fifth angel (MT) fifth
42. Rev. 16:12 - (TR) sixth angel (MT) sixth
43. Rev. 16:14 - (TR) of the earth and (MT) *omitted* [w]
44. Rev. 21:2 - (TR) I, John, saw (MT) I saw
45. Rev. 21:4 - (TR) God (MT) He
46. Rev. 21:15 - (TR) and the wall (MT) *omitted*
47. Rev. 22:6 - (TR) God of the holy prophets (MT) God of the spirits of the prophets

---

[v] This part of the verse is part of the quote of Exod. 19:12-13
[w] MT seems more correct unless earth is eretz (land of Israel)

Ancient Word of God

This list shows where the MT omits or changes a word in the Greek text that probably *does* change doctrine.

1. Matt. 3:11 - (TR) and with fire (MT) *omitted*
2. Matt. 10:8 - (TR) raise the dead (MT) *omitted*
3. Matt. 12:35 - (TR) heart (MT) *omitted*
4. Matt. 27:35 - (TR) that it might be fulfilled which was spoken by the prophet, they parted My garments among them, and upon My vesture did they cast lots. (MT) *omitted*[x]
5. Mark 12:32 - (TR) there is one God (MT) He is one
6. Mark 15:3 (TR) but He answered nothing (MT) *omitted*
7. Luke 9:23 - (TR) daily (MT) *omitted*
8. Luke 17:36 - (TR) Two men shall be in the field; the one shall be taken, and the other left. (MT) *omitted*
9. John 8:9 - (TR) being convicted by their own conscience (MT) *omitted*
10. Acts 7:37 - (TR) Him shall ye hear. (MT) *omitted*[y]
11. Acts 8:37 - (TR) And Philip said, If thou believest with all thine heart, thou mayest. And he answered and said, I believe that Jesus Christ is the Son of God. (MT) *omitted*[z]
12. Acts 9:5 - (TR) it is hard for thee to kick against the pricks. (MT) *omitted*
13. Acts 9:6 - (TR) And he trembling and astonished said, Lord, what wilt thou have me to do? And the Lord said unto him [aa] (MT) *omitted*

---

[x] Both TR and MT record this in John 19:24 and it is quoted by Tertullian *Jews 10*, AD 190

[y] Both TR and MT have this in Matt. 17:5 which is quoting Deut. 18:5

[z] MT is missing all of Acts 8:37; but it is quoted by Irenaeus *AH 3.12.8*, AD 170

[aa] Quoted by Apostolic Constitutions 8.5

14. Acts 10:6 - (TR) he shall tell thee what thou oughtest to do. (MT) *omitted*
15. Acts 13:23 - (TR) Jesus (MT) *omitted*
16. Acts 15:34 - (TR) Notwithstanding it pleased Silas to abide there still. (MT) *omitted* [bb]
17. Acts 24:7 - (TR) But the chief captain Lysias came upon us, and with great violence took him away out of our hands. (MT) *omitted* [cc]
18. Acts 24:8 - (TR) Commanding his accusers to come unto thee (MT) *omitted* [dd]
19. Romans 13:9 - (TR) Thou shalt not bear false witness (MT) *omitted*
20. 2 Corinthians 1:6 - (TR) and whether we be afflicted, it is for your consolation and salvation. (MT) *omitted*
21. Colossians 1:14 - (TR) through His blood (MT) *omitted*
22. Hebrews 2:7 -(TR) and didst set him over the works of Thy hands: (MT) *omitted*
23. 1 John 2:23 - (TR) but he that acknowledgeth the Son hath the Father also. (MT) *omitted*
24. 1 John 5:7-8 - [ee] (TR) the Father, the Word, and the Holy Ghost: and these three are one. And there are three that bear witness in earth (MT) *omitted*
25. Rev 1:11 - (TR) I am Alpha and Omega, the first and the last: (MT) *omitted*
26. Rev. 5:14 - (TR) and worshipped Him that liveth forever and ever. (MT) worshipped
27. Rev. 6:11 - (TR) to be fulfilled. (MT) complete their course.
28. Rev. 11:17 - (TR) which art, and wast, and art to come [ff] (MT) *omitted*

[bb] MT is missing all of Acts 15:34
[cc] MT is missing all of Acts 24:7
[dd] Finishing Acts 24:7
[ee] Quoted by Cyprian *Unity 1.6*, AD 250

29. Rev. 13:10 - (TR) He that leadeth into captivity shall go into captivity (MT) If anyone has captivity, he goes away
30. Rev. 14:8 - (TR) is fallen, is fallen [gg] MT fallen
31. Rev. 15:2 - (TR) and over his mark (MT) *omitted*
32. Rev. 18:2 - (TR) is fallen, is fallen (MT) *omitted*
33. Rev. 19:15 - (TR) winepress (MT) fierceness
34. Rev. 21:3 - (TR) and be their God (MT) *omitted*
35. Rev. 21:6 - (TR) it is done (MT) *-omitted*
36. Rev. 21:24 - (TR) of them which are saved (MT) *omitted*
37. Rev. 22:18 - (TR) shall (MT) may add plagues
38. Rev. 22:19 - (TR) shall (MT) may take away
39. Rev. 22:19 - (TR) book of life (MT) tree of life

This list shows where the MT adds something not found in the TR.

1. Matt. 27:41 - Pharisees
2. Luke 10:22 - And turning to His disciples He said
3. Rev. 7:9 - (long) white robes
4. Rev. 8:7 - and a third of the earth was burned up
5. Rev. 4:11 - our Lord and God, the Holy One
6. Rev. 10:5 - (right) hand
7. Rev. 11:16 - (throne) of God
8. Rev. 13:14 - (my own people) who dwell on the earth
9. Rev. 14:1 - (His name and) the name of His Father
10. Rev. 14:4 - These were redeemed (by Jesus)
11. Rev. 14:8 - (second) angel
12. Rev. 19:12 - (having names written) Just seems wrong
13. Rev. 19:15 - (double-edged) sword
14. Rev. 20:2 - he who deceives the whole world

[ff] The Beza quote, as it is called, was quoted in its entirety by Origin *OFP 1.2.10* about AD 240.
[gg] "Is fallen, is fallen" is the quote from Isaiah 21:9

15. Rev. 20:14 - the second death, (the Lake of Fire)
16. Rev. 21:14 - names of the (twelve) apostles

B.
Critical Text vs. Received Text

The Critical Text is composed of readings based on the Sinaiticus and other Alexandrian-type texts. Here are a few of the texts that have been accepted over the years. Remember, Westcott and Hort started with the Sinaiticus and others have corrected their text so that we now have the twenty-seventh edition of the Nestle-Aland Greek Text. Acts is 15% smaller in the Critical Text than in the Received Text. So the Critical Text Bible you read may have more (or less) of the changes.

1. Psalm 19:13 - (Heb) presumptuous sins (LXX) the alien
2. Matt. 6:13 - (TR) for Thine is the kingdom, and the power, and the glory, forever. Amen. (CT) *omitted*
3. Matt. 12:47 - (TR) Then one said to Him, Behold, Thy mother and Thy brethren stand without, desiring to speak to Thee. (CT) *omitted*
4. Matt. 17:21 - (TR) Howbeit this kind goeth not out but by prayer and fasting. (CT) *omitted*
5. Matt. 18:11 - (TR) For the Son of man is come to save that which was lost. (CT) *omitted*
6. Matt. 21:44 - (TR) And whosoever shall fall on this stone shall be broken: but on whomsoever it shall fall, it will grind him to powder. (CT) *omitted*
7. Matt. 23:14 - Woe unto you, scribes and Pharisees, hypocrites! for ye devour widows' houses, and for a pretence make long prayer: therefore ye shall receive the greater damnation. (CT) *omitted*

8. Mark 7:16 - If any man have ears to hear, let him hear. (CT) *omitted*
9. Mark 9:29 - (TR) prayer and fasting. [hh] (א, B) prayer
10. Mark 9:44 - (TR) Where their worm dieth not, and the fire is not quenched. (CT) *omitted*
11. Mark 9:46 - (TR) Where their worm dieth not, and the fire is not quenched. (CT) *omitted*
12. Mark 10:21 - (TR) take up the cross (CT) *omitted*
13. Mark 11:26 - (TR) But if ye do not forgive, neither will your Father which is in heaven forgive your trespasses. (CT) *omitted*
14. Mark 13:14 - (TR) spoken of by Daniel the prophet [ii] (CT) *omitted*
15. Mark 15:28 - (TR) And the Scripture was fulfilled, which saith, And He was numbered with the transgressors. (CT) *omitted*
16. Mark 16:9-20 (TR) *included* (CT) *omitted*
17. Luke 2:33 - (TR) Joseph (CR) father
18. Luke 17:36 - (TR) Two men shall be in the field; the one shall be taken, and the other left. (CT) *omitted*
19. Luke 22:43 - (TR) And there appeared an angel unto Him from heaven, strengthening Him. (CT) *omitted*
20. Luke 22:44 - (TR) And being in an agony He prayed more earnestly: and His sweat was as it were great drops of blood falling down to the ground. (CT) *omitted*
21. Luke 23:17 - (TR) For of necessity he must release one unto them at the feast. (CT) *omitted*
22. Luke 23:45 - (TR) the sun was darkened (א, B, C) the sun was eclipsed
23. John 1:18 - (TR) only begotten Son (CT) only begotten God

---

[hh] Fasting is included in the Byzantine text and p^{45}.
[ii] Matthew 24:15 proves this should be included

24. John 4:42 - (TR) the Messiah (CT) *omitted*

25. John 5:4 - (TR) For an angel went down at a certain season into the pool, and troubled the water: whosoever then first after the troubling of the water stepped in was made whole of whatsoever disease he had. (CT) *omitted*

26. John 7:8 - (TR) not up yet (CT) not[jj]

27. John 8:3-11 adulterous woman (TR) included (CT) *omitted*

28. Acts 8:37 - (TR) And Philip said, If thou believest with all thine heart, thou mayest. And he answered and said, I believe that Jesus Christ is the Son of God. (CT) *omitted* [kk]

29. Acts 9:5 - (TR) it is hard for thee to kick against the pricks. (CT) *omitted*

30. Acts 9:6 - (TR) And he trembling and astonished said, Lord, what wilt thou have me to do? And the Lord said unto him [ll] (CT) *omitted*

31. Acts 10:30 - (TR) prayer and fasting [mm] (א, B) prayer

32. Acts 15:34 - (TR) Notwithstanding it pleased Silas to abide there still. (CT) *omitted*

33. Acts 24:7 - (TR) But the chief captain Lysias came upon us, and with great violence took him away out of our hands. (MT) *omitted* [nn]

34. Acts 28:29 - (TR) And when he had said these words, the Jews departed, and had great reasoning among themselves. (CT) *omitted*

35. Rom. 11:6 - (TR) But if it be of works, then is it no more grace: otherwise work is no more work. (CT) *omitted*

36. Rom. 14:10 - (TR) judgment seat of Christ (CT) of God

[jj] Jesus saying He will not go, then going later, makes Him a liar. Saying He will not go *yet*, then going later solves this problem.

[kk] CT is missing all of Acts 8:37; but it is quoted by Irenaeus *AH 3.12.8*, AD 170

[ll] Quoted by Apostolic Constitutions 8.5

[mm] Fasting is included in the Byzantine text, p^{50}, and Dionysius (c. 265).

[nn] CT is missing all of Acts 24:7

37. Rom. 16:24 - (TR) The grace of our Lord Jesus Christ be with you all. Amen (CT) *omitted*
38. 1 Corinthians 7:5 - (TR) fasting and prayer (א, B) prayer
39. 1 Corinthians 15:51 - (TR) we shall not all sleep, but we shall all be changed (א, B, C) we shall all sleep, but we shall not all be changed[oo]
40. Eph. 3:9 - (TR) by Jesus Christ (CT) *omitted*
41. Col. 1:14 - (TR) through His blood (CT) *omitted*
42. 1 Tim. 3:16 - (TR) God (CT) who
43. 1 John 4:3 - (TR) Jesus Christ is come in the flesh (CT) *omitted*
44. 1 John 5:7-8 (TR) the Father, the Word, and the Holy Ghost: and these three are one. And there are three that bear witness in earth, (CT) *omitted*
45. Rev. 5:10 - (TR) us, we (CT) them
46. Rev. 21:24 - (TR) of them which are saved (CT) *omitted*
47. Rev. 22:19 (TR) book of life (CT) tree of life

In all, the word "Jesus" is omitted seventy times and the word "Christ" is omitted twenty-nine times from various passages in the Critical Text.

[oo] 1 Thessalonians 4 explains the doctrine of "changing," so we know the Alexandrian text has it backwards.

C.

Dead Sea Scrolls and Nag Hammadi

The Dead Sea Scrolls produced and protected by the Essene community at Qumran show us a godly library. In contrast, the Gnostic Scrolls produced by the Gnostic Egyptians in Nag Hammadi is the epitome of a satanic library.

Qumran - The Dead Sea Scrolls

Qumran has Scripture, commentaries, and cultic books (astrological) just as any good minister would have for the purpose of getting his facts straight and witnessing.

In the commentaries the phrase "it is written" often appears. Anyone who carefully studies this will see that phrase is only applied to what they know to be the true Scripture. It is never applied to any other type of writing, even their own community rule! This lets us know they believed in the inspiration of Scripture and tells us which books they considered to be Scripture.

You may hear some say that the Dead Sea Scrolls included the Apocrypha or that only about 40 to 60 percent of the Dead Sea Scrolls agree with the Received Text. This is true if we lump all the scrolls together. If we remove the commentaries, paraphrases, Greek texts, cult witnessing scrolls, and the like, we will see the same Old

Testament we have today. About 98% of those Dead Sea Scrolls agree with the Received Text. See the chart at the end of this chapter.

Nag Hammadi - The Gnostic Scrolls

In contrast, the Gnostic cults of that day rejected the true Scripture replacing the ancient Word of God with made-up nonsense. Anyone who has ever read any of their works will quickly conclude it is nonsense. They have been described as the writings of a childlike mind on drugs. The doctrines expressed in these works contradict, not only the Scriptures, but themselves as well!

Compare the reverence for the Scripture of Qumran with the fake texts of Nag Hammadi in the following charts.

The Dead Sea Scrolls

True Scripture
  The whole Old Testament
  except Esther (to date)
 	
Commentaries
  Habakkuk, Hosea, Isaiah,
  Micah, Nahum, Psalms, Song
  of Solomon, and Zephaniah
 	
Paraphrases
  Genesis, Exodus LXX [g],
  Exodus, Joshua, Leviticus [TRG],
  Job [TRG]
 	
Prophecy
  Damascus Document
  The Instruction
  Messianic Anthology
  Messianic Apocalypse
  Melchizedek fragment
  Midrash on the Last Days
  The Mysteries
  MMT
  The New Jerusalem [a]
  Priestly Prophecy
  Son of God Apocalypse [a]
 	
Other
  Book of War, Jubilees, Sirach,
  Tobit, Baruch [g]
  Testaments of Levi [a], Judah [a],
  Naphtali [a], Joseph [a]
	Community Related
	  Calendrical Document
	  Community Rule Scroll
	  Copper Scroll
	  Festival Prayers
	  Temple Scroll
	  Thanksgiving Hymns
	  Three Tongues of Fire
	  Rule of Blessing
	  Rule of the Congregation
	  Songs of King Jonathan
	  Songs of Sabbath Sacrifice
	  Songs of the Sage
	  War Scroll
	
	Cults of their Day
	  Allegory of the Vine
	  Apocryphon of Moses
	  Apocryphon of David
	  Apocryphon of Malachi
	  Apocryphon on Samuel-Kings
	  Book of Giants
	  Book of Noah
	  Enoch [a], Enoch [g]
	  Genesis Apocryphon [a]
	  Words of Michael the
	    Archangel

[a] Aramaic; [TRG] Targum; [g] Greek; Hebrew is unmarked

The Gnostic Scrolls

Fake Gospels	Other
Gospel of the Egyptians*	Allogenes
Gospel of Philip	Asclepius 21-29
Gospel of Thomas	Authoritative Teaching
Gospel of Truth	Concept of Our Great Power
	Dialogue of the Savior
Fake Epistles	Discourse on the Eighth and
Acts of Peter	Ninth
Acts of Peter and the twelve	Eugnostos the Blessed
Apostles	Exegesis on the Soul
Book of Thomas the Contender	Hypostasis of the Archons
Letter of Peter to Philip	Hypsiphrone
Prayer of the Apostle Paul	Interpretation of Knowledge
Teachings of Silvanus	Marsanes
	On the Origin of the World
Fake Apocalypses	Paraphrase of Shem*
Adam , James (1st), James	Plato, Republic 588A-589B
(2nd), Paul, Peter	Second Treatise of the Great
	Seth
Fake Prophecy	Sentences of Sextus
Apocryphon of James	Sophia of Jesus Christ
Apocryphon of John	Testimony of Truth
Melchizedek	Thought of Norea
	Three Steles of Seth
Community Related	Thunder, Perfect Mind
On the Anointing	Treatise on the Resurrection
On the Baptism A	Trimorphic Protennoia
On the Baptism B	Tripartite Tractate
On the Eucharist A	A Valentinian Exposition
On the Eucharist B	Zostrianos
Prayer of Thanksgiving	

* Mentioned by the church fathers as official Gnostic literature and very
wicked.

D.

Other Language Bibles

	Date	Luke 2:33	1 Tim. 3:16	1 John 5:7-8
Received Text	**95**	**Joseph**	**God**	**-included-**
Gr. Orthodox	?	Joseph	God	-included-
Old Syriac	150	Joseph	God	-included-
Old Latin	157	Joseph	God	-included-
Italic	157	Joseph	God	-included-
Vaudois	120	Joseph	God	-included-
Gallic	177	Joseph	God	-included-
Goth	350	Joseph	God	-included-
Armenian	400	Joseph	God	-included-
Palestinian	450	Joseph	God	-included-
Sahidic	180	father	who	-omitted-
Bohairic	200	father	he	-omitted-
ℵ and B	350	father	who	-omitted-
Peshita	400	Joseph	which	-omitted-*
Vulgate	400	father	which	-omitted-*

*Some copies include the passage but most omit it.
The Gallic Bible was created in southern France. There are still 1244 copies of the Armenian Bible in existence. The Vaudois is the ancient Waldensian Bible. The Sahidic has John 1:1 as "the word was *a* god."

Modern Bibles that were based on the same text as the ancient Bibles listed above are: the French (Oliveton) Bible of 1535, the Czech Bible of 1602, the Italian (Diodati) Bible of 1606, and the Official Greek Bible used from apostolic times to the present day by the Greek Orthodox Church.

All the above-mentioned Bibles and the vast majority (about 98%) of the 5300 extant New Testament manuscripts are in agreement with the Received Text.

As an example, the legend behind the Vaudois Bible is that missionaries from Antioch came about AD 120 to help them translate a New Testament into their own language. Later, more missionaries came from Antioch and the Old Testament was finished by approximately AD 180. The Vaudois Bible contains the whole Old Testament. It does not include the Apocrypha, which they were told was never meant to be a part of the Old Testament. Their New Testament is the same exact twenty-seven books we have today plus Paul's letter to the Laodiceans. The New Testament text is virtually the same (no missing verses) as the Received Text. This same story with slight variations is told by most of the peoples who have the ancient Bibles listed above. Here are quotes from both John Wesley and Jonathan Edwards showing they were aware of the ancient history of the Waldensians and their ancient Bible.

"It is a vulgar mistake, that the Waldenses were so called from Peter Waldo of Lyons. They were much more ancient than him; and their true name was Vallenses or Vaudois from their inhabiting the valleys of Lucerne and Agrogne. This name, Vallenses, after Waldo appeared about the year 1160, was changed by the Papists into Waldenses, on purpose to represent them as of modern original." John Wesley *Notes on the Revelation of John,* 13:6, p. 936.

"Some of the popish writers themselves own that this people never submitted to the Church of Rome. One of the popish writers, speaking of the Waldenses, says, the heresy of the Waldenses is the oldest heresy in the world. It is supposed that they first betook themselves to this place among the mountains, to hide themselves from the severity of the heathen persecutions which existed before Constantine the Great." *The Works of Jonathan Edwards Vol. 4, Work of Redemption. 3*

The following chart shows how the Received Text was kept by the Greek Orthodox Church and translated into the old languages, while the corrupted Egyptian Gnostic texts (Alexandrian) were translated into the Vulgate and the Critical Text Bibles.

None of the old Latin and old Syriac are missing any verses; they all include 1 John 5:7. There are over 20,000 manuscripts from all the old languages, most of which have never been cataloged. Those that have been are all found to be based on the Received Text, with the exception of the Old Coptic, called Sahidic.

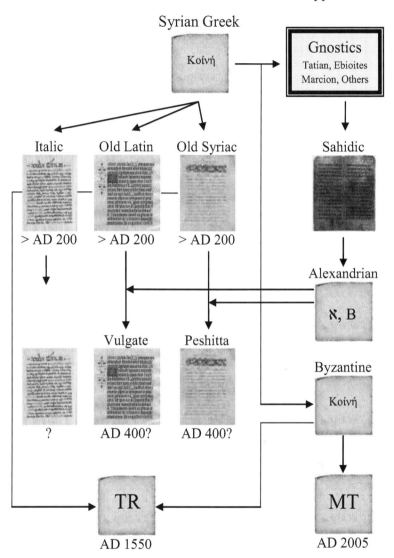

E.
Alphabetical Master Bible List

2

142		2001 Translation	2001
113	KJ21	21st Century King James	1991

A

189	ANT	Accurate New Testament	2008
130	AKJV	American King James Version	1999
34	ASV	American Standard Version	1901
48	AAT	An American Translation	1935
89	BECK	An American Translation	1976
69	AMP	Amplified Bible	1965
132	ALT	Analytical-Literal Translation	1999
175	ARTB	Ancient Roots Translinear Bible	2006
29	Anderson	Anderson's 1865 New Testament	1865
119	AST	Anointed Standard Version	1995
16	Quaker	Anthony Purver Bible	1764
152	ABP	Apostolic Bible Polyglot	2003
157	AB	The Apostles' Bible	2004
57	TANT	The Authentic New Testament	1955
177	AVU	Authorized Version Update	2006
176	AV7	AV7 (New Authorized Version)	2006
214	Szasz	Awful New Testament (Emery Szasz)	-

B

75	BNT	(William) Barkly New Testament	1968
61	BV	The Berkeley Version	1958
183	TB	The Besorah (plagiarized '98 version)	2008
53	BBE	Bible in Basic English	1949
87	LivEng	The Bible in Living English	1972
76	BWE	Bible in Worldwide English (NT)	1969
78	TBR	The Bible Reader	1969

28		Emphatic Diaglott	1864
211	Jubilee	English Jubilee 2000 Bible	-
151	EMTV	English Majority Text Version	2003
140	ESV	English Standard Version	2001
111	EVD	English Version for the Deaf	1989
23	Etheridge	Etheridge's Peshitta	1849
201	EB	Expanded Bible	2011

F

153	FNT	Faithful New Testament	2003
213	FAA	Far Above All Version	-
197	TFB	The Free Bible	2010
147		A Fresh Parenthetical Translation (NT)	2002

G

7		Geneva	1560
37	Godbey	Godbey New Testament	1902
90	GNB	Good News Bible	1976
110	GNC	God's New Covenant (NT)	1989
117	GW	God's Word	1995
5		Great Bible	1537
99	LITV	Green's Literal Translation	1985

H

159	HRV	Hebraic-Roots Version	2004
205	HNV	Hebrew Names Version	-
156	HCSB	Holman Christian Standard Bible	2004
38	Fenton	The Holy Bible in Modern English	1903
68	HNB	Holy Name Bible	1963
148	HNC	Holy New Covenant	2002
187	HOB	Holy Orthodox Bible	2008
58	HSM	Holy Scriptures of the Masoretic Text	1955
141	HSV	Holy Scriptures Version	2001

I

120	AIV	An Inclusive Version	1995
91	IB	Interlinear Bible (Green)	1976
181	ICB	International Children's Bible	2007
210	ISV	International Standard Version	-

J

46	MNT	James Mofatt	1926
71	JB	Jerusalem Bible	1966
107	JNT	Jewish New Testament	1989
42	JPS	Jewish Publication Society of America Ver.	1917
20	JST	Joseph Smith's Translation	1830
31	Julia	Julia E. Smith Parker Translation	1876

K

135	KJV2000	King James 2000 Version	2000
81	KJII	King James II	1971
10	KJV	King James Version	1611
139	KJVER	King James Version Easy Reading	2001
101	KIT	Kingdom Interlinear Translation	1985
167	KJ3	KJ3—Literal Translation Bible	2005
82	KJV20	KJV Twentieth Century Version	1971
59	KLNT	Kleist-Lilly New Testament	1956
56	Knox	Knox Translation of the Vulgate	1955

L

47	Lamsa	Lamsa Bible	1933
133		The Last Days New Testament	1999
195	LEB	Lexham English Bible	2010
26	Leeser	Leeser Bible	1853
171		Life with God Study Bible	2005
83	TLB	The Living Bible	1971
85	TLB-CE	The Living Bible Catholic Edition	1971
22	LONT	Living Oracles New Testament	1835

M

11	Mace	Mace New Testament	1729
209	MGB	The Manga Bible	-
4		Matthew	1537
104	MCT	McCord's New Testament	1988
145	MSG	The Message	2002
215	MASV	Modern American Standard Version	-
44	MRB	Modern Reader's Bible	1923
129	MKJV	Modern King James Version	1999
77	MLB	Modern Language Bible	1969
199	MLV	Modern Literal Version	2011
25	Murdock	Murdock's Peshitta	1852

N

96		A New Accurate Translation	1984
182	NIBEV	Natural Israelite Bible, English Version	2007
80	NAB	New American Bible	1970
198	NABRE	New American Bible Revised Edition	2011
86	NASB	New American Standard Bible	1971
165	NCPB	New Cambridge Paragraph Bible	2005
113	NCV	New Century Version	1991
79	NEB	New English Bible	1970
164	NET	New English Translation	2005
179	NETS	New English Translation of the Septuagint	2007
186	NHEB	New Heart English Bible	2008
194	NIV10	NIV 2010	2010
92	NIV	New International Version	1978
121	NIrV	New International Reader's Version	1996
122	NIVI	New International Inclusive Language	1996
97	NJB	New Jerusalem Bible	1985
98	NJPS	New Jewish Publication Society of America	1985
95	NKJV	New King James Version	1982
124	NLT	New Living Translation	1996
103	NLV	New Life Version	1986
105	NRSV	New Revised Standard Version	1989
106	NRSV-CE	New Revised Standard Version Catholic Ed.	1989
162	NSB	New Simplified Bible	2004
123		The New Testament (Lattimore)	1996
49	Greber	The New Testament	1937
30	Noyes	New Testament	1869
73		The New Testament: A New Translation	1968

18		New Testament in an Improved Version	1808
54	NWT	New World Translation	1950
66	NNT	Noli New Testament	1961
64	NSNT	Norlie's Simplified New Testament	1961

O

193	OEB	Open English Bible	2010
100	ONT	Original New Testament	1985
146	OJB	Orthodox Jewish Bible	2002
180	OSB	Orthodox Study Bible	2007

P

60	PME	Phillips New Testament in Modern English	1958

R

128	RcV	Recovery Version	1999
170		Renovaré Spiritual Formation Bible	2005
88	SNB	Restoration of Original Sacred Name Bible	1976
208	RNKJV	Restored Name King James Version	-
108	REB	Revised English Bible	1989
137	RKJNT	Revised King James New Testament	2000
55	RSV	Revised Standard Version	1952
72	RSV-CE	Revised Standard Version Catholic Edition	1966
32	RV	Revised Version	1885
43	RNT	Riverside New Testament	1923
35	EBR	Rotherham's Emphasized Bible	1902

S

166	SN-KJ	Sacred Name King James Bible	2005
94	SSBE	Sacred Scriptures, Bethel Edition	1981
136	SSFOY	Sacred Scriptures, Family of Yah Edition	2000
127	TS98	The Scriptures '98 Version	1998
93	SEB	Simple English Bible	1980
51	SPC	Spencer New Testament	1941

178		Spirit of Prophecy Study Bible	2006
84	TSB	The Story Bible	1971
160	TSNT	The Source New Testament	2004

T

188	TNB	Tarish Nephite Bible	2008
6		Taverner	1539
125	TMB	Third Millennium Bible	1998
19	Thm	Thomson's Translation	1808
115	TEV	Today's English Bible	1992
163	TNIV	Today's New International Version	2005
216	TEB	Transparent English Bible	-
202	TrLB	Tree of Life Bible	2011
36	TCNT	The Twentieth Century New Testament	1902
2		Tyndale NT	1526

U

173	UVNT	Understandable Version NT	2005
114	Gaus	Unvarnished New Testament	1991
134	UKJV	Updated King James Version	2000
191	UPDV	Updated Version	2009
143	UTV	Urim Thummim Version	2001

V

217		The Victorious Gospel of Jesus Christ New Covenant Translation	-
185		The Voice	2008
154	VW	A Voice In The Wilderness Holy Scriptures	2003

W

17		Wakefield New Testament	1791
21	Webster	Webster's Revision	1833
15	Wesley	Wesley's New Testament	1760
41	WVSS	Westminster Version of the Sacred Scriptures	1913
39	WNT	Weymouth NT	1904
12	Whiston	Whiston's Primitive New Testament	1745

172	WNT	William's New Testament	2005
50	WmNT	William's New Testament	1937
149	TWOY	The Word of Yahweh	2003
203	WEB	World English Bible	-
204	WEB-ME	World English Bible Messianic Edition	-
192	WGCIB	Work of God's Children Illustrated Bible	2010
40	WAS	Worrell New Testament	1903
63	WET	Wuest Expanded Translation	1961
1		Wycliffe	1382
144	WV	Wycliffe Version (Noble)	2001

Y

27	YLT	Young's Literal Translation	1862
212	YRT	Young's Revised Translation	-
161	Younan	Younan's Peshitta Interlinear	2004

Other Books by
Ken Johnson, Th.D.

Ancient Post-Flood History
Historical Documents That Point to a Biblical Creation.

This book is a Christian timeline of ancient post-Flood history based on Bible chronology, the early church fathers, and ancient Jewish and secular history. This can be used as a companion guide in the study of Creation Science.

Some questions answered: Who were the Pharaohs in the times of Joseph and Moses? When did the famine of Joseph occur? What Egyptian documents mention these? When did the Exodus take place? When did the Kings of Egypt start being called "Pharaoh" and why?

Who was the first king of a united Italy? Who was Zeus and where is he buried? Where did Shem and Ham rule and where are they buried?

How large was Nimrod's invasion force that set up the Babylonian Empire, and when did this invasion occur? What is Nimrod's name in Persian documents?

How can we use this information to witness to unbelievers?

Ancient Seder Olam
A Christian Translation of the 2000-year-old Scroll

This 2000-year-old scroll reveals the chronology from Creation through Cyrus' decree that freed the Jews in 536 BC. The *Ancient Seder Olam* uses biblical prophecy to prove its calculations of the timeline. We have used this technique to continue the timeline all the way to the reestablishment of the nation of Israel in AD 1948.

Using the Bible and rabbinical tradition, this book shows that the ancient Jews awaited King Messiah to fulfill the prophecy spoken of in Daniel, Chapter 9. The Seder answers many questions about the chronology of the books of Kings and Chronicles. It talks about the coming of Elijah, King Messiah's reign, and the battle of Gog and Magog.

This scroll and the Jasher scroll are the two main sources used in Ken's first book, *Ancient Post-Flood History*.

Ancient Prophecies Revealed
500 Prophecies Listed In Order Of When They Were Fulfilled

This book details over 500 biblical prophecies in the order they were fulfilled; these include pre-flood times though the First Coming of Jesus and into the Middle Ages. The heart of this book is the 53 prophecies fulfilled between 1948 and 2008. The last eleven prophecies between 2008 and the Tribulation are also given. All these are documented and interpreted from the Ancient Church Fathers.

The Ancient Church Fathers, including disciples of the twelve apostles, were firmly premillennial, pretribulational, and very pro-Israel.

Ancient Book of Jasher
Referenced in Joshua 10:13; 2 Samuel 1:18; 2 Timothy 3:8

There are thirteen ancient history books mentioned and recommended by the Bible. The Ancient Book of Jasher is the only one of the thirteen that still exists. It is referenced in Joshua 10:13; 2 Samuel 1:18; and 2 Timothy 3:8. This volume contains the entire 91 chapters plus a detailed analysis of the supposed discrepancies, cross-referenced historical accounts, and detailed charts for ease of use. As with any history book, there are typographical errors in the text but with three consecutive timelines running though the histories, it is very easy to arrive at the exact dates of recorded events. It is not surprising that this ancient document confirms the Scripture and the chronology given in the Hebrew version of the Old Testament, once and for all settling the chronology differences between the Hebrew Old Testament and the Greek Septuagint.

Third Corinthians
Ancient Gnostics and the End of the World

This little known, 2000-year-old Greek manuscript was used in the first two centuries to combat Gnostic cults. Whether or not it is an authentic copy of the original epistle written by the apostle Paul, it gives an incredible look into the cults that will arise in the Last Days. It contains a prophecy that the same heresies that pervaded the first century church would return before the Second Coming of the Messiah.

Ancient Paganism
The Sorcery of the Fallen Angels

Ancient Paganism explores the false religion of the ancient pre-Flood world and its spread into the gentile nations after Noah's Flood. Quotes from the ancient church fathers, rabbis, and the Talmud detail the activities and beliefs of both Canaanite and New Testament era sorcery. This book explores how, according to biblical prophecy, this same sorcery will return before the Second Coming of Jesus Christ to earth. These religious beliefs and practices will invade the end time church and become the basis for the religion of the Antichrist. Wicca, Druidism, Halloween, Yule, meditation, and occultic tools are discussed at length.

The Rapture
The Pretribulational Rapture of the Church Viewed From the Bible and the Ancient Church

This book presents the doctrine of the pretribulational Rapture of the church. Many prophecies are explored with Biblical passages and terms explained.

Evidence is presented that proves the first century church believed the End Times would begin with the return of Israel to her ancient homeland, followed by the Tribulation and the Second Coming. More than fifty prophecies have been fulfilled since Israel became a state.

Evidence is also given that several ancient rabbis and at least four ancient church fathers taught a pretribulational Rapture. This book also gives many answers to the arguments midtribulationists and posttribulationists use. It is our hope this book will be an indispensable guide for debating the doctrine of the Rapture.

Ancient Epistle of Barnabas
His Life and Teaching

The Epistle of Barnabas is often quoted by the ancient church fathers. Although not considered inspired Scripture, it was used to combat legalism in the first two centuries AD. Besides explaining why the Laws of Moses are not binding on Christians, the Epistle explains how many of the Old Testament rituals teach typological prophecy. Subjects explored are: Yom Kippur, the Red Heifer ritual, animal sacrifices, circumcision, the Sabbath, Daniel's visions and the end-time ten-nation empire, and the temple.

The underlying theme is the Three-Fold Witness. Barnabas teaches that mature Christians must be able to lead people to the Lord, testify to others about Bible prophecy fulfilled in their lifetimes, and teach creation history and creation science to guard the faith against the false doctrine of evolution. This is one more ancient church document that proves the first century church was premillennial and constantly looking for the Rapture and other prophecies to be fulfilled.

The Ancient Church Fathers
What the Disciples of the Apostles Taught

This book reveals who the disciples of the twelve apostles were and what they taught, from their own writings. It documents the same doctrine was faithfully transmitted to their descendants in the first few centuries and where, when, and by whom, the doctrines began to change. The ancient church fathers make it very easy to know for sure what the complete teachings of Jesus and the twelve apostles were.

You will learn, from their own writings, that the first century disciples taught about the various doctrines that divide our church today. You will learn what was discussed at the seven general councils and why. You will learn who were the cults and cult leaders that began to change doctrine and spread their heresy and how that became to be the standard teaching in the medieval church. A partial list of doctrines discussed in this book are:

Abortion	Free will	Purgatory
Animals sacrifices	Gnostic cults	Psychology
Antichrist	Homosexuality	Reincarnation
Arminianism	Idolatry	Replacement theology
Bible or tradition	Islam	Roman Catholicism
Calvinism	Israel's return	The Sabbath
Circumcision	Jewish food laws	Salvation
Deity of Jesus Christ	Mary's virginity	Schism of Nepos
Demons	Mary's assumption	Sin / Salvation
Euthanasia	Meditation	The soul
Evolution	The Nicolaitans	Spiritual gifts
False gospels	Paganism	Transubstantiation
False prophets	Predestination	Yoga
Foreknowledge	premillennialism	Women in ministry

Ancient Book of Daniel

The ancient Hebrew prophet Daniel lived in the fifth century BC and accurately predicted the history of the nation of Israel from 536 BC to AD 1948. He also predicted the date of the death of the Messiah to occur in AD 32, the date of the rebirth of the nation of Israel to occur in AD 1948, and the Israeli capture of the Temple Mount to take place in AD 1967! Commentary from the ancient rabbis and the first century church reveals how the messianic rabbis and the disciples of the apostles interpreted his prophecies.

Daniel also indicated where the Antichrist would come from, where he would place his international headquarters, and identified the three rebel nations that will attack him during the first three-and-a-half years of the Tribulation.

Ancient Epistles of John and Jude

This book provides commentary for the epistles of John and Jude from the ancient church fathers. It gives the history of the struggles of the first century church. You will learn which cults John and Jude were writing about and be able to clearly identify each heresy. You will also learn what meditation and sorcery truly are. At the end of each chapter is a chart contrasting the teaching of the church and that of the Gnostics. Included are master charts of the *doctrine of Christ*, the *commandments of Christ*, and the *teaching of the apostles*.

Learn the major doctrines that all Christians must believe:

Jesus is the only Christ	The Rapture
Jesus is the only Savior	Creationism
Jesus is the only begotten Son of God	Eternal life only by Jesus
Jesus is sinless	The sin nature
Jesus physically resurrected	Prophecy proves inspiration
Jesus will physically return to earth	Idolatry is evil
God is not evil	

Ancient Messianic Festivals
And The Prophecies They Reveal

The messianic festivals are the Biblical rituals God commanded the ancient Israelites to observe. These ancient rites give great detail on the first coming of the Messiah including the date on which He would arrive, the manner of His death, and the birth of His church. You will also learn of the many disasters that befell the Jews through the centuries on the ninth of Av. The rituals speak of a Natzal, or rapture of believers, and a terrible time called the *Yamin Noraim*. They give a rather complete outline of this seven-year tribulation period, including the rise of a false messiah. They also tell of a time when the earth will be at peace in the Messianic Kingdom. In addition to the seven messianic festivals, you will learn the prophetic outline of other ceremonies like Hanukkah, the new moon ceremony, the wedding ceremony, the ashes of the red heifer, and the ancient origins of Halloween. You will also learn of other prophetical types and shadows mentioned in the Bible.

Bibliography

Brenton, The Septuagint with Apocrypha, Hendrickson, 1986

Ken Johnson, Ancient Prophecies Revealed, Createspace, 2008

Eerdmans Publishing, Ante-Nicene Fathers, Eerdmans Publishing, 1886

Cruse, C. F., Eusebius' Ecclesiastical History, Hendrickson Publishers, 1998

Philip Schaff, Companion to the Greek Testament, London MacMillan, 1833

Ken Johnson, Ancient Church Fathers, Createspace, 2010

Michael Maynard, The Debate Over 1 John 5. 7-8, Comma Publications, 1995